Cowley Publications is a ministry of the brothers of the

Society of Saint John the Evangelist, a monastic order in

the Episcopal Church. Our mission is to provide books

and resources for those seeking spiritual and

theological formation. Cowley Publications is

committed to developing a new generation of writers

and teachers who will encourage people to think and

pray in new ways about spirituality, reconciliation, and

the future.

Song of the Shepherd

Community of Divine Love
617 W. Roses Rd.
San Gabriel, CA 91775
www.communityofdivinelove.com

Song of the Shepherd

∾ *Meeting the God of Grace in Psalm 23*

TONY HORSFALL

Cowley Publications
Cambridge, Massachusetts

Text copyright © 2004 Tony Horsfall

Original edition published in English under the title *Song of the Shepherd* by The Bible Reading Fellowship, Oxford, England

Copyright © The Bible Reading Fellowship 2004

Library of Congress Cataloging-in-Publication Data

Horsfall, Tony.
  Song of the Shepherd : meeting the God of grace in Psalm 23 / Tony Horsfall.
    p. cm.
  Includes bibliographical references.
  ISBN 1-56101-274-2 (pbk. : alk. paper)   1. Bible. O.T. Psalms XXIII—Criticism, interpretation, etc. 2. God—Biblical teaching. 3. Christian life—Biblical teaching.   I. Title.
  BS145023rd .H67 2005
  223'.206—dc22

                                        2004030479

Cover design: Brad Norr Design
Interior design and production: Andrew MacBride

Cowley Publications
4 Brattle Street
Cambridge, Massachusetts 02138
800-225-1534   www.cowley.org

Affectionately dedicated to my friends in Singapore, especially:

Alan Chew, who had the faith to publish my first book,
and has opened many doors of opportunity for me;

Grace Lim, Alfred Quah, Teo Soo Hoong, Stephen Looi,
Henry and Pansy, and Simon and Rinda, all of whom have
welcomed and appreciated some foreign "ginger"!

CONTENTS

FOREWORD

All of my life has been a search for authentic Christianity—not the quasi-religious stuff of formula or methods, but Christianity that works in time of need as well as blessing. As a songwriter with various degrees of success, I've sought to mirror these aspirations through the songs I've written down the years. They have served as milestones to me as I've traveled along life's path. There's something about the combination of lyrics and melody when they work together that is truly wonderful, as they draw the listener or participant into a shared expression of praise to our Creator.

David was a worshiper. In the stillness of the night or under the heat of the midday sun, he would serenade his God from the hills. As king of Israel he ushered in a whole new musical order and structure to declare praise to God throughout the land. It was innovative and radical. Four thousand musicians with festive shouts, songs, and extravagant joy stood in stark contrast to the worship expression of the tabernacle of Moses, where reverential silence was the norm. Well beyond the public gaze, David never forgot what it was to bare his soul to his maker, producing a remarkable outpouring of prayers and petitions to the God he first discovered as a shepherd boy on the hills. David's heart was drawn again and again to worship. The legacy of his writings and longings recorded in the Psalms has proved a priceless treasure trove of comfort, praise, and encouragement for Christians down through the centuries, spanning all cultures and continents.

Many of the Psalms in biblical times were also set to music. Obviously the musical style and idiom were quite different from our accepted contemporary forms, but I would be intrigued to know what musical score David would have chosen in today's culture for Psalm 23, his magnificent description of faith. Would it have been written in a minor key to highlight the elements of mystery disclosed here? Or perhaps something grander, emphasizing the trustworthy Shepherd leading us to a triumphant finale on our journey of faith? Maybe it would have been set in a blues style depicting the valley experiences of life. I can only speculate and wonder, but I am sure that it would have moved me to worship.

As well as being an outstanding musician, David proved himself a skilful wordsmith. Seeking to make tangible what he knew about his God, we can be sure that just as he chose five smooth stones for the task in hand many years before, when he risked his life to face Goliath, the words for this enduring psalm are expertly chosen. When accurately applied, they have the potential to slay the Goliaths of fear, exhaustion, and anxiety that so often daunt us in our own lives.

I'm so pleased to write this foreword for my good friend Tony Horsfall. With his vast experience of Christian ministry, Tony has much wisdom to share. He knows and understands that the essence of our life in God is found at the place of surrender and devotion to Jesus. Caught up in technicalities and academic studies, we can have a tendency to worship at the altar of doctrinal correctness instead of humbly at our Savior's feet. Christ-centered and grace-focused, Tony writes with passion and insight, using Psalm 23 as a backdrop to describe the journey of faith with its subtle balance of activity and rest. Honoring the lyrical flow of this most famous psalm, he skillfully highlights different facets of the good Shepherd's character and kindness. Here is a book that encourages us, with David of old, to walk with God, to trust his heart, and to worship him.

Dave Bilbrough, international
songwriter and worship leader

INTRODUCTION

We have lived in our present house for almost twenty years. Soon after we moved in, we bought a picture to hang over the fireplace in the lounge. It is an early morning scene in the countryside, with trees and grass, a lake, and the sun just beginning to rise. The soft and mellow colors, the gentle browns, greens, and yellows, create a feeling of tranquility. People who visit us often comment on the painting and the peaceful atmosphere it gives to the room.

It occurred to me recently, however, that while other people often notice it, I hadn't really "seen" the picture for ages. Of course I see it every day, but I hadn't really looked at it properly in a long time. So I took a moment to sit down and let my eyes feast on its beauty once again. It was like having a new painting, such was the impact it made on me as I considered it afresh.

I feel a little like this about Psalm 23. Of all the psalms written by King David, the anointed psalmist of Israel, this must be the most popular and well known. Perhaps because it is so familiar there is a danger that we miss its beauty and fail to receive the impact of its message. I realized recently myself that I had never really looked at it in any detail. I discovered that in almost thirty years of preaching and teaching, I had never spoken even once from this passage. I guess I assumed that if everyone knew the psalm so well, they would be tired of it, and anyway, what more was there to say? What could I add to what others had already said?

For some reason, however, I turned to it again a few months ago, and began to study it properly for the very first time. I was amazed at what I found there! It was like discovering a new part of scripture altogether as the Holy Spirit unfolded it before my eyes.

I began to see that this picture of the shepherd and the sheep speaks very profoundly about the precious relationship we can have with God. Nothing is more important to us as we seek to live the Christian life than to develop our relationship with God, understanding exactly who he is and what he offers to do for us. Here we are invited into a relationship of intimacy and grace, a secure place where we can find peace and contentment like nowhere else.

I saw it, too, as an invitation to share life's journey with the God of grace. Life is often compared to a journey. There are stages and phases that we must each pass through as we move from the cradle to the grave, transitions that take us from one period of life to another. Sometimes the journey is geographical as we move from place to place; sometimes it is more emotional and psychological as we grow and mature and develop.

The Christian life can also be seen as a journey, a pilgrimage taking us deeper into God in order to discover more and more of his love for us. We feel it too as we step out in obedience to his commands in the adventure of faith, seeking the outworking of his will in our daily lives.

What Psalm 23 teaches us is that, throughout this journey, we can depend on the companionship and help of a God who is at heart the God of grace. This means that he loves us dearly and without condition. He longs to do good to us and to supply us with everything we need to make it to the end. He has our best interests at heart and is completely reliable.

I noticed further that this psalm deals with some of the major issues for those of us who are disciples—learning to rest, learning to trust God in the darker moments of life, and learning to live out of God's resources, not our own. The gracious God who is our Shepherd has an agenda for each of our lives. Life is not a series of random and meaningless events if we are his. He is leading us and guiding us, bringing us through circumstances and events that will draw us closer to himself and make us more like him. This is his ultimate goal for every disciple. We need to understand what he is doing in our lives at any moment, and this psalm reveals to us some of the most significant lessons he will teach us as we journey together with him.

Since my own fresh encounter with Psalm 23, its message has been a constant theme in my teaching and preaching, and also as I have led Quiet Days and retreats. I have been amazed at the response to it, and its timely relevance for the world in which we live.

How to Use This Book

I can see many different ways to use this book, either individually or together with others. You could read it as the basis for your own daily time with God, perhaps taking a chapter every couple of days and using it for your own meditation. I hope you will find here lots to stimulate further thought and prayer. At the end of each of the four main sections there are questions that will help you to reflect on what you have read and apply what you are learning to your own situation. You may like to use a journal, writing down your responses and noting other insights that come to you as you reflect.

I have mentioned already how I have used Psalm 23 in the setting of Quiet Days and retreats. This is the kind of book that you can take away with you when you go on vacation, or when you are having a few days to be still and to seek God. It is not a heavy theological tome, but is written with the hope that those who read it will be drawn closer to God in simple, loving devotion. I'm sure that is the purpose David had in mind too when he penned these beautiful words.

It would make an ideal resource for a group study as well. Perhaps over a two-week period, individuals could read one of the sections themselves, and then when the group meets, they could share their responses to the group questions which are also included. The material is ideal for nurturing a group of new Christians, as it covers many of the key issues in discipleship—God's provision and protection, understanding guidance, finding a balanced lifestyle, coping with trials, receiving strength from God, living in the Spirit, even how to face death and dying. It will also be helpful as a refresher course for more mature believers because it touches on some of the main concerns of those who have been on the journey a little longer.

Churches could also make it the foundation of a sermon series, with home and cell groups following up what is being taught week by week, with discussion in more intimate settings. This is how we have used the material in my own church, and we benefited enormously from studying this great psalm in such detail.

However you choose to use this book, I pray that you will begin to rediscover this very familiar part of scripture for yourself and that the Holy Spirit will open your heart to the treasures it contains.

I trust that as you read and reflect, you will be enriched in every way as you engage with the inspired word of God, and that you will encounter not just the psalm, but the Shepherd as well.

PART 1

Building a Relationship

The Lord is my shepherd, I shall not be in want. (v. 1)

ભ

Successful relationships do not just happen. They come about because people invest in them—taking the time and trouble to work at them, to get to know each other, to become closer. The same is true of our relationship with God.

1 A Shepherd's Song

David was a superstar within his own generation. As a young man, his exploits in battle, especially against the Philistines, gave him the status of a folk hero. His rise to prominence, and eventually to the throne, was welcomed by all. Handsome, articulate, and brave, he was the popular choice to become leader of the nation.

David was also a skilful musician, a warrior with a poet's imagination and sensitive spirit. It was his ability to play the harp that first brought him to Saul's attention and to the royal court. His gentle melodies and comforting lyrics soothed the spirit of the troubled king. Throughout his life David continued to compose his songs, expressing in words and melody the deepest feelings of his heart, and reflecting the ebb and flow of his faith during the turbulent times through which he lived.

This man with a heart after God was the one chosen by God to lead the nation of Israel. For this task, he had been anointed by the prophet Samuel. The Holy Spirit was with him, and this anointing spilled over into his song writing. More than seventy of the Psalms (the hymnbook of ancient

Israel) are attributed to him personally, and in all probability it was David who first brought his own and other songs together in a compilation for the use of God's people in worship. Through his inspired compositions, Israel's beloved singer brought to his people a revelation of what God was like and how he was at work in their lives. In David's own experience of God they could see a reflection of their own (see 1 Samuel 16–17; 2 Samuel 23:1–7).

Of all the psalms that David penned, none is more popular than Psalm 23. We may turn to Psalm 139 for a wonderful exposition of the knowledge that God has about us, or to Psalm 51 when we have sinned and feel the need to be forgiven; to Psalm 27 when we seek guidance, or to Psalm 34 when are discouraged or afraid. Many psalms will be appreciated because they meet specific needs, and we will have other favorite pieces, but it is to Psalm 23 that we fondly turn again and again.

Here we find comfort and strength like nowhere else. Here we discover the joy of a personal relationship with a God who cares for us unreservedly. Here we find the basis for hope and confidence even in the darkest of times. It is a favored portion of the word of God, breathing into the reader's spirit the calm and serenity of which it speaks. These are inspired words, loved by all generations, in all cultures and at all times. Of this ancient songwriter's many beautiful pieces, Psalm 23 is without doubt the greatest and most abiding. It is King David's greatest hit!

This particular psalm describes the personal relationship between David and his Lord, and in so doing sets forth a pattern for anyone who believes in God. If the Lord is David's Shepherd, he can be mine. If he cares for David in this way, he will also care for me in a similar way.

The picture of a shepherd is one of the most personal images used for God in the Old Testament. It is different from speaking of him as a rock or fortress or hiding place. It conveys a note of caring, of intimacy, of belonging. Next to the term *Father,* it is the warmest and most comforting of all the descriptions of God.

David uses personal pronouns throughout the psalm. Although, in Hebrew, the little word *my* is no more than a suffix on the noun *shepherd*, what an important emphasis it provides! The care of this particular Shepherd is related to the needs of the individual sheep. It is helpful when reading the psalm to notice these personal pronouns (he, me, you, my) because, as Martin Luther once said, "The heart of religion lies in its personal pronouns." These little words create a sense of belonging to God, of being known by him, of being important and significant. They indicate an intimate relationship, indeed a covenantal relationship that binds Shepherd and sheep together.

Scholars are uncertain as to the background of the psalm. It could fit any period of David's life. Some suggest that it comes from early in his life, during the period when he worked as a shepherd boy. Sitting out on the hills day after day, he had plenty of time to meditate and pray, and the link between his own care for the sheep and God's care of him would naturally have been formed in his mind.

Others say that the psalm is more the product of mature thinking, and may have been written toward the end of David's life, when he was looking backwards and reflecting on the way that God had led and guarded and kept him.

Some go so far as to specify a particular context for the psalm—that period when David was on the run from his son Absalom (see 2 Samuel 15 onwards). The suggestion is that, while he was a fugitive, David was forced to turn again to God for help, and to re-evaluate his relationship with God. Success and prosperity may have caused him to grow spiritually cold, but the crisis of Absalom's rebellion forced him to seek God again, and to remember the closeness and intimacy he had enjoyed as a boy. It was then that a new song was formed in his mind and heart, a song of confidence in the God of grace who remained his Shepherd.

It is difficult to say with certainty exactly when the psalm was written, or what its setting was. What we can say is that David is writing out of both his own intimate knowledge of God and his familiarity with the life of a shepherd. It is a shepherd's song, written by a shepherd, about a Shepherd. He is describing a personal relationship with a personal God, and as such the psalm is a constant reminder to us that this is the kind of relationship to which God invites us.

This is not a psalm about abstract concepts or lofty theology. It is rooted in the realities of everyday needs and concerns. Its great appeal lies in its accessibility to the ordinary person. Poetic it may be, and full of imagery, but it remains simple and straightforward, dealing with issues that concern us all.

It speaks of wants and needs and things we lack. It talks about rest and relaxation, food and drink, contentment and peace, friendship and acceptance. It addresses such issues as loneliness, overcoming fear, knowing what's right to do, making good choices. It touches on painful subjects like bereavement and loss, the mystery of evil, the question of suffering. It helps us to cope with life and make sense of what is happening to us, to look death in the face with confidence. Joy and sadness are here; so too are celebration and conflict. Above all, it reminds us that we are not alone.

With great skill and craft, David weaves all these issues together with an economy of words but in a beauty of language that is captivating to both heart and mind. The changing scenes of life are reflected in the changing moods of the psalm—from the tranquility of rest by quiet waters to the turmoil, uncertainty, and fear of shadowy darkness, to the happy celebration of friendship and hospitality around the banqueting table. Holding it together is the constant theme, the headline thought, the bottom line: "The Lord is my shepherd." He is our provider and protector, our companion and guide, our comforter and friend. Whatever our need and whatever our circumstance, he is there, and he is everything we need.

Unlike many other psalms, this song remains positive throughout. There are no angry outbursts against the wicked, no dark moods of depression, no questioning of God. Neither are there petitions or requests—no beseeching of God to do something special. It is simply a declaration of all that God is, and an affirmation of all that he desires to be toward us in our need. It is an expression of one man's faith in a God whom he believes to be both good and gracious, and in it he becomes the mouthpiece for everyone who chooses to live by faith.

The emphasis throughout is on God as provider, and the human being as receiver. It is therefore a psalm of grace, and calls us into a grace-based relationship with God—that is, a relationship where the initiative is with God, who freely and without any obligation chooses to meet us at our point of need. The flow of such a relationship is always from God to humanity. Every verse of the psalm illustrates this truth—God giving, man or woman receiving. Our Shepherd is also our friend, and he calls us to sit at the table he has prepared in advance for us. He invites us to come and take our place, and enjoy his abundant provision. That is grace, and grace is the abiding foundation of our relationship with God. Psalm 23 sounds the note of grace as clearly as anywhere else in scripture.

David was a man of joy, and joy is a rare and wonderful quality that creates in us a lightness of heart and a spirit of hope. It is the antidote to despair, and gateway to God's presence. David sang and was free. He reflected on the goodness and grace of God, and his heart was lifted above his cares and worries. Through his psalms, David teaches us to sing our own praise to God. They allow us to lift our heavy souls, to restore our wounded spirits, and to rise up in faith again.

No wonder, down the centuries, Psalm 23 has been the psalm most often set to music by the church, and sung with feeling in many different settings. It calls us to faith, to intimacy with God, to the experience of his nearness. It invites us to rest, to trust and not be afraid, to rejoice and be glad. As we speak or sing these beautiful words, their truth brings us again to God, and much-needed grace begins to flow into our lives.

This is the shepherd's song, and it is ours as well. God is the Shepherd, and we are the sheep, the sheep of his pasture. And of this we are truly glad.

2 The Lord Is the Shepherd

Given the pastoral nature of life in ancient Israel, we should not be surprised to find that God uses imagery taken from this aspect of their everyday world to communicate with his people. By declaring himself to be their Shepherd, God was reaching deep into the psyche of the people of Israel, a people who from the very beginning of their existence had been pastoral nomads. The special relationship that exists between shepherd and sheep was well known to them: it was something they felt and knew instinctively. They were surrounded by living examples of the interaction between shepherd and sheep. The significance of God's self-revelation would not be lost on any of them.

Those of us living in the urban environment characteristic of the twenty-first century have to work a little harder at understanding and appreciating the pastoral imagery used in Psalm 23. Even for those of us who are more aware of rural life, and sheep farming in particular, there remains a gap in our understanding. We are not so intimately connected to pastoral life, and there are significant differences between shepherding in the ancient Near East and modern-day sheep farming as many of us observe it. Nevertheless, the scriptures are so full of shepherd–sheep imagery that we can quickly transport ourselves back into biblical times and use our imaginations to see what truths lie behind the metaphor.

Although David is credited with writing Psalm 23, the picture of God as a shepherd actually goes back much further in time to Jacob, one of the patriarchs of the nation of Israel. All the patriarchs kept flocks, and shepherding was part of their way of life, crucial to their survival. When the time comes to pray a blessing over his grandchildren (Joseph's sons, Ephraim and Manasseh), it is natural for Jacob to look back over his own life and pray to the covenant-keeping God who has been with him throughout—"the God who has been my shepherd all my life to this day" (Genesis 48:15).

Jacob's words describe how he perceived and understood his relationship to God. He saw himself in a personal relationship with a God who was leading and guiding him on life's journey, and who was gently watching over him in the way a shepherd would watch over his sheep. His life was not a random series of chance events or haphazard occurrences. No, there was meaning and purpose to it, because God was leading him. Looking back, he can see the Shepherd shaping the events of his turbulent life, and this is the same blessing that he now prays for his grandchildren.

The thought of God shepherding or leading his people occurs repeatedly throughout the Old Testament story. At no point in the history of Israel were the people more convinced of God's shepherding activity than during the exodus, that great event when Moses led them out of slavery in Egypt. It may have been only with hindsight that they could see it, but Israel's prophets always interpreted this great deliverance as a divine act—an intervention by the Shepherd of Israel.

The psalm writer Asaph, for instance, places this interpretation on those formative events: "But [God] brought his people out like a flock; he led them like sheep through the desert. He guided them safely, so they were unafraid; but the sea engulfed their enemies" (Psalm 78:52–53). And again he says, "You led your people like a flock by the hand of Moses and Aaron" (Psalm 77:20).

Asaph's understanding is of a God who is intimately involved with his people, leading and guiding them even through difficulties and dangers, and in the presence of their enemies. Some scholars see many echoes of the events of this period in Psalm 23. Indeed, if we read the passage with the exodus and wilderness wanderings in mind, it is not difficult to see that Israel's own history provides a suitable backdrop for David's writing.

Later prophets continued to see evidence of the shepherding activity of God on behalf of Israel. The period of the exile was a painful time of chastening for the nation, but God did not abandon them. Even there they could see his hand at work, and feel his shepherd's heart. Jeremiah looks forward to a day when Israel will return to her own land: "He who scattered Israel will gather them and will watch over his flock like a shepherd" (Jeremiah 31:10). Again, "I myself will gather the remnant of my flock out of all the countries where I have driven them and will bring them back to their pasture, where they will be fruitful and increase in number" (Jeremiah 23:3).

Isaiah, with the exile in mind, sees the Lord tenderly bringing the people back, sensitive to their needs, carefully leading them home like the good Shepherd he is: "He tends his flock like a shepherd: he gathers the lambs in his arms and carries them close to his heart; he gently leads those that have young" (Isaiah 40:11).

Ezekiel contrasts the faithful care of God with that of the faithless leaders of Israel. God will not abandon his people at their moment of need, or think only of his own self-interest. "I myself will search for my sheep and look after them. As a shepherd looks after his scattered flock when he is with them, so will I look after my sheep. I will rescue them from all the places where they were scattered on a day of clouds and darkness" (Ezekiel 34:11–12).

Whether in the exodus, or in the return from exile, the gracious activity of God can be seen. Israel did not deserve such care and attention. God responded to them from the grace within his own heart, and out of the covenant relationship that he had established with them, not because of any merit on their part. Not surprisingly, "Shepherd of Israel" became a favorite name for God, and the inspiration behind many heartfelt cries for help at other times: "Hear us, O Shepherd of Israel, you who lead Joseph like a flock . . . Awaken your might; come and save us" (Psalm 80:1–2).

What, then, can we say about a God who describes himself as a shepherd? What is he like, and what does he do? Everything in Psalm 23 is in keeping with the sheep-lore of the day, with good practice, as we would call it now. There is nothing that contradicts the real life of a shepherd with his sheep. This is why the psalm is best understood through the eyes of David's own experience as a shepherd.

Clearly a shepherd is a person with considerable skill and knowledge of his craft. It takes generations of understanding, handed down from one family member to another, to make a good shepherd, and years of personal experience out in the field before an individual really knows the sheep. Fortunately God has that kind of understanding of each of us because he made us and knows us individually. We are the sheep of his pasture, and he knows us through and through.

A shepherd must be both brave and strong—strong because he is often alone in rugged and remote places, in all kinds of weather, and brave because he must protect his flock from wild animals and robbers. At the same time he must be tender and gentle—able to care for his flock, tending the ones that are sick or injured, helping those that are weak or lame. How blessed we are to have a God who is strong enough to help us in need, yet gentle enough to feel our pain and our hurt!

A shepherd must have a good heart, one that puts the needs of his flock above his own self-interest. He must not be harsh or brutal with the sheep, and must be willing to expose himself to danger in order to find any that have gone missing. Personal sacrifice is inevitable for a shepherd who truly cares for his flock. The character of God is such that, without hesitation, we would call him a good shepherd. Everything we know of him speaks of his commitment to us and his willingness to lay down his life for us.

Most importantly, the shepherd must be able to lead his flock, guiding them to find rich pasture and refreshing water. He is responsible to provide for them. He is their guide who goes before them, leading the way. The God we worship is a God who can be trusted. We can safely commit our lives to him and know that he will guide us in the right paths. With him as our leader we shall never go astray, and with him as our guide we shall lack for nothing.

So what does the shepherd do? He leads, he provides, he protects, he cares. And what is he like? He is skillful, brave, tender, and wise. These are the activities and attributes of the Lord who is our Shepherd. With him by our side, we can be content.

3 Jesus the Good Shepherd

We cannot read the words of Psalm 23 without thinking of Jesus. From our perspective we can see that David is speaking prophetically here: in speaking about the Shepherd, he is in fact looking forward to the coming of the Messiah. Jesus made this connection clear and plain when he identified himself as the fulfillment of this very scripture. Boldly he declared, "I am the good shepherd" (John 10:11). His earthly life became a visible demonstration of what David was saying. In Jesus, the divine Shepherd took human form and entered our world, bringing the psalm quite literally to life.

Throughout the Old Testament, there was a longing for the day when God would send a Savior, the Messiah. The person who would come is described in various ways, but within this prophetic hope and anticipation is the longing for one who would shepherd the people of Israel.

Ezekiel bore witness to this desire. Angered and frustrated by the religious and political leaders of his day, he compares them to false shepherds who take care only of themselves and who exploit the flock for their own ends. He confidently expects God's intervention to save his people and to hold these abusive leaders accountable. Ultimately he reaches forward to the day when the true leader will appear, born of David's line and being a true son of David. "I will place over them one shepherd, my servant David, and he will tend them; he will tend them and be their shepherd" (Ezekiel 34:23).

Somewhat later, the prophet Micah shares a similar burden. He foresees the birth of a ruler who will be born in Bethlehem, one "whose origins are from of old, from ancient times." He goes on to be even more specific: "He will stand and shepherd his flock in the strength of the Lord, in the majesty of the name of the Lord his God. And they will live securely, for then his greatness will reach to the ends of the earth" (Micah 5:4). Clearly we recognize here a prophecy about both the place of the birth of Jesus (in Bethlehem) and the nature of his ministry (to be a shepherd).

Thus, when Jesus declares himself to be the good shepherd, he is making two important statements. First, he is saying that he is the fulfillment of this prophetic expectation. He is the long-awaited Messiah, the true Shepherd of Israel. Second, he is making a direct claim to divinity, since David had said, "The Lord is my shepherd": what Jesus is really saying is, "I am the one of whom David spoke." Certainly the nature of his claim was not lost on those who heard him, for some in the crowd were ready to stone him for blasphemy.

With this in mind, we can see that John 10 becomes the New Testament equivalent of Psalm 23. The teaching of Jesus here becomes his own inspired exposition and explanation of the words penned by David under the Spirit's anointing so much earlier. In particular, they help us to make this direct connection between the shepherd of the psalm and Jesus, and also to understand why he describes himself as the "good" shepherd. It is something he says twice, and with emphasis—literally, "I am the shepherd, the good (or excellent) one" (John 10:11, 14).

In what way is Jesus a *good* shepherd? He had rejected the ascription of good when the rich young ruler called him "good teacher," perhaps because he seemed to be using it too casually, especially since only God is truly good (Luke 18:19). If Jesus is now using it himself, therefore, it is because once more he is carefully and deliberately stating something about his identity. He is the good shepherd because he is God, and God is good.

Jesus' essential goodness is brought out in several ways in the passage in John 10. He is good in contrast to the thieves and robbers. This may refer to false teachers, especially the scribes and Pharisees who, with their legalistic brand of religion and proud self-righteousness, lead people astray and prevent them from receiving the life of God. They place heavy burdens on people and exploit their positions to their own advantage. In short, they are in it for what they can get out of it. They come only to steal and kill and destroy.

Jesus, as the good shepherd, is altogether different. He comes with the right credentials, having been born of God, and he comes to give not receive: "I have come that they might have life, and have it to the full" (John 10:10). Here we see most clearly the difference between mere religion and the grace-based relationship with God that David describes in Psalm 23 and that Jesus came to make available. Grace is all about giving. God wants to give and give and give. He delights in meeting our needs, and asks for nothing in return except a grateful heart and responsive life. He longs to impart his very own life to us, so that we do not just exist but truly come alive to God and all that he is doing in the world.

The good shepherd also stands in contrast to the stranger, who knows nothing of the sheep and has no relationship with them. Consequently, when the stranger calls to the sheep, they do not follow because they do not recognize his voice. How different with the good shepherd. He knows his sheep intimately, by name, and cares for them as individuals. When he calls, they respond because they know his voice. They trust him and will follow him gladly. Again we see the true nature of a grace-based relationship with God. The voice that calls us is always the voice of truth and love, always encouraging us, always building us up. The good shepherd never speaks harshly or to condemn or to wound. It is the devil whose voice is harsh and demanding, reminding us of sin and failure, speaking doom and gloom to our souls. The Shepherd speaks only words of life, bringing healing, forgiveness, acceptance, and hope.

The main reason, however, that we call our Shepherd good is because he willingly lays down his life for the sheep (John 10:11, 17–18). Here he is seen in contrast to the hireling or paid worker who cares nothing for the sheep because they do not belong to him. When trouble or danger comes, he runs away, abandoning the flock, for he thinks only of himself and his own safety.

How different is a true and good shepherd! He will never abandon his sheep, because he cares everything for them. He gives his life for them in sacrificial toil day after day, putting himself out to meet their needs. If they are lost, he goes out to find them, regardless of the weather and risk to himself. When we think of Jesus, of course, we know that he demonstrated his love for us by making the ultimate sacrifice, laying down his life for us on the cross to take away our sin. No one made him do it; he was under no obligation. He chose to lay down his life for us, voluntarily dying in our place. Here is grace indeed, and here is true goodness at work.

It is vitally important that we know and believe in our hearts that we have a good Shepherd. Our faith in the goodness of God can be undermined by evil and negative suggestions that he is unfair, unreliable, even unkind. God is none of those things. God is altogether good and deals with us always in grace. Faithful, reliable, consistent, true: these are the words that describe the one who is totally good.

How we think about God determines how we relate to him, especially in crisis or trouble. That is why counselor Selwyn Hughes says that it is essential that our primary view of God (the one we carry deep in our hearts) is accurate. If we think of him as a cruel, uncaring, distant figure, we shall not have much joy or peace of heart. If, on the other hand, we know him to be a tender-hearted, caring Shepherd who constantly watches over us in love, then we shall become more secure and relaxed in the way we live. The God we worship is a God of grace, and we can rest secure in the knowledge that he accepts us and delights in us.

There are other places in the New Testament where Jesus is identified as the Shepherd. Peter, for instance, describes him as the Shepherd and Overseer of our souls, to whom we have now returned after going astray (1 Peter 2:25). Peter also marks Jesus out as the Chief Shepherd, to whom under-shepherds like himself are accountable, from whom they take their example and inspiration and who, one day, will return: "And when the Chief Shepherd appears, you will receive the crown of glory that will never fade away" (1 Peter 5:4).

Those of us in leadership in churches and Christian organizations do well to examine our own leadership styles and personal motivation in the light of the example of Jesus. If we have been called to shepherd the people of God, we have a high privilege, and must serve in a way that resembles the way in which Jesus deals with us. Peter reminds us that we must serve willingly and humbly, not lording it over others, and not using our position for financial gain.

Another important passage is in the book of Hebrews. Here, in a beautiful doxology that brings this great epistle to a close, we are introduced to Jesus as the Great Shepherd. "May the God of peace, who through the blood of the eternal covenant brought back from the dead our Lord Jesus, that great Shepherd of the sheep, equip you with everything good for doing his will, and may he work in us what is pleasing to him, through Jesus Christ, to whom be glory for ever and ever. Amen" (Hebrews 13:20–21).

Here we see that not only did the Shepherd die for our sins, but God has also brought him back to life. A dead shepherd might be an inspiration to us, but could do nothing practical to help us on our journey through life. A living shepherd is altogether different. He is able to accompany us as we journey and to impart his life and strength to us. As the writer says, he equips us with gifts of grace, and then empowers us with the grace to do his will.

Devotional writers have often pointed to the special setting of Psalm 23. It follows on from Psalm 22, which describes the crucifixion in vivid detail. Here we meet the Good Shepherd and encounter his cross. Then comes Psalm 23 with its emphasis on a living relationship with a living Savior. This is the Great Shepherd, and we are comforted by his rod and his staff (crook). Afterward comes Psalm 24, with its magnificent portrayal of the ascended Christ, who reigns on high and who will soon return. Here he is the Chief Shepherd, and the one who wears a crown.

Good Shepherd, Great Shepherd, Chief Shepherd: these are the titles given to Jesus linking him for ever with David's psalm. They tell us who he is, and what he is about. Nor are they merely abstract notions. He wants to be who he is, especially in his relationship with his people. He longs to become all of these things to us in the context of our daily lives.

4 All We Like Sheep

If God is like a shepherd, David is implying that we are like sheep. Indeed, Psalm 23 is written from the perspective of a sheep, and David seems to have no problem with identifying himself in this way, even though it is not the most flattering of comparisons. Lambs may be cute and cuddly, but sheep are among the most dim-witted and helpless of creatures. That, of course, is why they need a shepherd. I am aware that some studies claim that sheep are actually very intelligent animals, but I remain to be convinced. The Bible, at any rate, suggests that even if they are clever, they are not always very wise.

In various ways the Bible draws out this comparison between the behavior of sheep and that of human beings. According to one shepherd, there are so many similarities between people and sheep, it is embarrassing! If we are to relate properly to God, it is important that we understand not only what he is like, but also what we are like. Self-awareness is an essential ingredient in relationships, and understanding ourselves is vital for spiritual growth and development. In particular, we need to have a realistic assessment of human nature.

In what ways, then, are we like sheep?

Isaiah the prophet makes a penetrating analysis of our human condition when he says this: "We all, like sheep, have gone astray, each of us has turned to his own way" (Isaiah 53:6). One thing for certain is that sheep have an inbuilt capacity to wander and get lost. They seem to get themselves into trouble without really trying. If there is a hole to fall into, they will fall into it; if there is a bush to get tangled in, they will find it; if there is a cliff edge nearby, they will head in that direction. Perhaps something of the exasperation of the shepherd in the light of the foolishness of his sheep can be felt in the words of Jesus when he was teaching one day. "If any of you has a sheep," he said, "and it falls into a pit on the Sabbath, will you not take hold of it and lift it out?" (Matthew 12:11). Obviously he is speaking about a very common experience with which he assumes many of his hearers would easily identify. The hapless plight of a lost sheep would not be difficult for them to picture.

What Isaiah is saying is that we share this inbuilt tendency to wander and get lost. It is part of our fallen human nature to drift away from God, choosing to go our own way and do what we want. By nature we are selfish and stubborn, preferring self-determination to the will of God. The result is that often we make bad choices and fall into "holes" of our own making. This was the painful experience of the prodigal younger son in the parable that Jesus told (Luke 15). His selfish determination to have his own way and break free from the restrictions of home turned out to be his downfall. His life fell apart simply through his own foolishness. He could well have echoed the words of Psalm 119:176: "I have strayed like a lost sheep."

Isaiah's description is an inclusive one. What he says is true of every one of us, of you and of me. We need to be aware of the tendency to self-destruct latent within every human heart. Even after conversion, when the power of sin has been broken in our lives (Romans 6:6), the potential to wander remains, for we still battle against temptation. That is why hymn writer Robert Robinson (1735–90) puts it like this: "Prone to wander—Lord, I feel it; prone to leave the God I love." He knew the vagaries of his own heart, and did not trust himself. Rather he learned, as we must all learn, to put his confidence in the keeping power of the Shepherd.

Another interesting comparison comes from Jesus himself. On one occasion he looked out over the crowds who had come to him for help and healing, and his heart filled with compassion, for he saw that they were "harassed and helpless, like sheep without a shepherd" (Matthew 9:36). No one has ever shown more insight into human nature than Jesus.

Sheep that have no shepherd soon lose direction and wander round aimlessly. They run here and there in a mindless panic. With no one to protect them, they become prey to wild animals, and with no one to care for them they are vulnerable to disease and pests. They become both harassed (plagued by difficulties) and helpless (unable to do anything about it). How readily this speaks to our human condition. Left to live our lives on our own, we become both confused and aimless. We cannot make sense of life, and lack the kind of purpose that would give us meaning and direction. Bruised and wounded by the hard knocks that come our way, we search frantically for any form of relief, grateful for any crumb of comfort to ease the pain in our hearts. A quiet desperation often lies behind the measured image we present to the world.

Matthew 9:36 records that Jesus was deeply moved at this point. Eugene Peterson's paraphrase, *The Message*, says that when Jesus looked over the crowd "his heart broke." What can a shepherd do when he sees the sheep scattered and dispersed? Instinctively he wants to gather them together, to bring them into the safety of his fold, to protect them and provide for them. In the broken world of today, his desire remains the same.

The apostle Peter adds a third strand to the comparison we are making between sheep and human beings. Sheep are the most defenseless of animals. They have no sharp teeth with which to defend themselves, no claws with which to attack. No one runs when a sheep bleats. They cannot move quickly and are easily caught. Consequently they are prey to other wild animals—lions, bears, wolves, and so on. In the same way, we human beings are weak and helpless when it comes to the spiritual enemies that array themselves against us. Peter puts it like this: "Be self-controlled and alert. Your enemy the devil prowls around like a roaring lion looking for someone to devour" (1 Peter 5:8). The devil is always seeking to catch us out in some unguarded moment, in order to tempt us to sin, heap condemnation upon us, oppress our spirits, and gain some advantage over us. Left to ourselves, we are no match for him and his cunning, and have no strength against the demonic powers that serve his purpose. We need the help and protection of someone greater than ourselves—a good Shepherd.

Perhaps Peter was speaking here from first-hand experience, for he had learned the hard way about his own vulnerability. At the time when Jesus was arrested, Peter had boasted in his self-confidence that even if everyone else fell away, he certainly would not (Matthew 26:33). He was willing to go to prison or even to die (Luke 22:33). His bravado quickly disappeared, however, when the moment came and he was questioned concerning his association with Jesus. Even the words of a mere servant girl unnerved him, and his confidence melted. Three times he denied his Lord. When Jesus turned and looked at him, his heart broke as he remembered the Master's words of caution and his own foolhardiness (Luke 22:56–62). Satan had indeed sifted him like wheat, as Jesus had warned him (Luke 22:31). It was a painful but abiding lesson. From that point on, Peter was aware of his own vulnerability. It made him depend all the more on Jesus, to be alert to the activity of the devil. From the wisdom of experience he now seeks to help those younger in the faith to avoid the pitfall of boastful self-confidence.

Taking care of sheep is no easy matter. They repeatedly wander and get lost. They cannot look after themselves. They are weak and vulnerable. Why bother? Only a shepherd can explain the love he feels for his flock and the commitment he has to them.

Only grace can explain why Jesus the good Shepherd continues to care for us. In the face of our repeated rebellions and stubborn refusal to do his will, he goes on loving us. Despite our continuing need of his help and understanding, and our inability to do what is right, he remains faithful to us. Even knowing our propensity to fail and let him down, he never gives up on us. He continues to rescue us, repeatedly binds up our wounds, daily watches over us. With infinite patience and endless compassion he sticks with us, when he could justifiably give up on us. His mercy knows no limits, his love no boundary.

This is why we love him in return. Anyone who looks back over the checkered history of their own walk with God cannot but marvel at his faithfulness and constancy. Anyone who knows their own heart, and their own human weakness, cannot but be amazed at the persevering love of the good Shepherd. But it does continue, and that is the essence of grace, and the source of our confidence.

For it is not my hold on him that matters, but his hold on me.

5 Shepherd and Sheep

We have looked already at the Shepherd, and also considered the sheep. Now it is time to bring the two together, for shepherd and sheep are meant to be one, and rightly belong together. When we see a shepherd, we expect to see sheep; and when we see sheep, we expect to see a shepherd. A special relationship exists between them, and illustrates for us many aspects of our own relationship with God.

When David so confidently affirms, "The Lord is my shepherd," he is looking at this relationship from the sheep's viewpoint. He is speaking about a relationship that is very personal and extremely important. What binds him to the Shepherd is his awareness of need and sense of dependency. Jesus, as the good Shepherd, can also speak about the relationship from his point of view, and again it is very personal and very important to him, for he says, "I know my sheep" (John 10:14). What binds him to the sheep is the bond of love that, as the owner of the sheep, he feels for each member of his flock. Thus, Shepherd and sheep are joined together in a relationship that to each of them is both intimate and meaningful.

Jesus illustrated this for us in the parable of the lost sheep (Luke 15:4–7). The shepherd, in counting his sheep, notices that one is missing. Leaving the ninety-nine behind, he goes off into the open country and searches until he finds it. Then, rejoicing, he returns home, calling friends and neighbors to party with him in celebration of his good fortune in finding the lost sheep. What the story teaches is the value of every single individual to God. They are his sheep, and therefore worth finding, no matter what the personal cost. It is this kind of attachment that forms the basis for the unique relationship between shepherd and sheep.

Throughout the Bible we read of God's desire to live in relationship with humankind. It is often expressed in the formula, "I will be their God, and they will be my people" (Leviticus 26:12; Hebrews 8:10). It is what we call a covenant relationship, the kind of relationship where two parties are intentionally joined together. Marriage is a good example of a covenant relationship, and is often used in scripture as one way to describe the relationship between God and his people. The bond between shepherd and sheep is another good example of a covenant relationship.

When we say "The Lord is my shepherd," we are reminding ourselves that we live in a special relationship with God. He has committed himself to us, and, as best we can, we give ourselves back to him. Of course, this is not a covenant between equals. It is a covenant where God is the senior partner, the one making the first move, initiating and sustaining the relationship, ensuring that it stays intact. It is a covenant of grace. Nevertheless, it is a two-way relationship in which our response is vital and sought after.

My own personal relationship with God began when I was fourteen years old. Although my parents were not church-goers, they encouraged me to attend Sunday school at the local Methodist chapel.

I only heard the gospel message, however, when some students from a nearby Bible college visited for a week of special meetings. For the first time (as far as I can remember) I heard that Christ died for my sins and that, if I welcomed him into my life, I could be saved. With tears rolling down my cheeks I responded to the opportunity to "receive" Christ.

Certainly at that moment I felt as if it was my choice to follow Jesus, and that everything rested on my decision. Indeed, one of the songs I quickly learned to sing said as much: "I have decided to follow Jesus." Only later, as I got to know the Bible better and understand the doctrine of salvation more fully, did I realize that my decision was, in fact, only my response to the prior movement of God in my life. It was God who was drawing me to himself and giving me the desire to respond. It wasn't so much that I was accepting Christ as that he was accepting me. The Shepherd had come searching for his lost sheep, and I had been found.

This movement of grace in our lives is the foundation of any genuine relationship with God. It is also what gives the relationship security, for it depends upon God and not upon us. I can say that he is mine because, first of all, I am his. He has taken hold of my life and brought me to himself. I belong to him, and therefore he belongs to me. What we have is a covenant of grace.

Salvation comes to us as a free gift, totally undeserved, and without the need for any merit on our part. "For it is by grace you have been saved, through faith—and this not from yourselves, it is the gift of God—not by works, so that no one can boast" (Ephesians 2:8–9). Just as we begin the Christian life in grace, so we are to continue living it out, depending on the movement of God's grace in our lives. "So then, just as you received Christ Jesus as Lord, continue to live in him, rooted and built up in him, strengthened in the faith as you were taught, and overflowing with thankfulness" (Colossians 2:6–7). God is committed to providing us with everything we need to keep our part of the relationship. He is at work within us, enabling us and empowering us to live the life to which he has called us.

Psalm 23 perfectly illustrates the grace that flows from shepherd to sheep. The sheep contribute nothing to the relationship. All they do is lie down, and follow where the shepherd leads! Their main responsibility is to listen for the shepherd's voice. All the responsibility lies with the shepherd. It is he who finds pasture and water. It is he who protects and guards the sheep. It is he who tends to their needs and fights off their enemies.

Such is the nature of our relationship with God. He has committed himself to us in a covenant relationship. He has undertaken to give us all that we need to live the Christian life. He has placed his love upon us and marked us out as his own. Nothing will ever change that. We are safe because he watches over us. Jesus said, "My sheep listen to my voice; I know them, and they follow me. I give them eternal life, and they shall never perish; no one can snatch them out of my hand" (John 10:27–28).

Does this make us casual in our approach to the Christian life? Not at all. What it does is to make us eternally grateful to the one who has loved us so much and been so gracious to us. Grace produces gratitude, and gratitude is one of the healthiest motivations of all. We love God because he first loved us. Forgiven much, we love much, and in turn forgive others. The more we receive from God, the more we want to give ourselves to him. Having received freely, we can give freely.

God stands before us as a God of grace. He has already made provision for us to be saved and, through the sacrificial death of his Son, to be able to enter into a personal relationship with himself. The Bible expression for this is "to be reconciled" (2 Corinthians 5:20), which means to be brought back into a harmonious relationship. It is important to make our own personal response to the grace that God offers to us, to receive the gift of salvation for ourselves. As we welcome Jesus into our lives as our Lord and Savior, we are brought into this wonderful personal relationship with God. Then we can say with assurance, "The Lord is my shepherd."

I was sharing the truths of Psalm 23 at a meeting in Singapore recently. It was a period of economic downturn, and many were feeling the pressure. The message of David's psalm seemed to strike a chord with many. Afterward an elderly Chinese gentleman came to speak with me and to ask for prayer. "I do not have any financial worries," he said, "but my heart is empty."

It was to satisfy the emptiness of our aching hearts that Jesus came. Just as my friend that day was introduced to the good Shepherd, so we can each find welcome and acceptance with the one who alone can meet the deepest needs of our hearts. It doesn't matter that we don't deserve it, or feel that we can't keep it up. He welcomes us on the basis of his free, unmerited favor. He promises to give us all that is required to live a new life.

His covenant of grace is everything we need.

6 Everything I Need

Many years ago I attended a Billy Graham crusade at which George Beverley Shea was the soloist. His rich, deep voice filled the stadium as he sang "The New Twenty-Third Psalm" by Ralph Carmichael. The opening words, based on the Living Bible, have stayed with me ever since as a powerful affirmation of faith and trust: "Because the Lord is my Shepherd, I have everything I need."

The first verse of Psalm 23 conveys a great sense of assurance and confidence. If it was written while David was on the run and in exile from Jerusalem, it is all the more remarkable that he should express such positive faith in the midst of trying circumstances. He is verbalizing what someone has called the "logic of grace"—that if it is true to say the Lord is my Shepherd, it follows with certainty that I will have everything that I need. The first is the guarantee of the second. If the one is true, then the other follows automatically.

We must be clear, though, about the exact meaning of this great affirmation. What are we saying when we so confidently declare that "I have everything I need" or "I shall not be in want"?

It does not mean that I have everything that I want. Obviously I do not always have everything in life that I would like to have. Advertisers know exactly how to take advantage of this gap and how to fuel within us a desire for something more or something else (usually their own product). Most of us are a bundle of wants, many of which are merely selfish desires, cravings driven by a consumer society and the result of the acquisitive streak that exists within each of us. Every parent has to learn to distinguish between what a child wants and what a child needs. The concern is not merely about what the child thinks he or she wants, but what is actually good for them, even if it means withstanding a tantrum in the supermarket. God does not always give us what we want or imagine we cannot do without. He is concerned for our highest good.

Neither does it mean that I have everything I think I need. We are not always able to discern our true needs. We may feel we need something, but God may see it differently. We may assume that we need something now, but God may deem that this is not the right time, and it is better to wait. We are more likely to be soft on ourselves, imagining we really need something immediately when God knows that we will grow far more in character and grace if the need is not satisfied at once. His wisdom and love combine to filter out the superficial needs from the genuine ones. What he does guarantee, however, is that those needs which are the most real (be they emotional, physical, material, or spiritual) will be satisfied. This is the confidence that we have, born out of the logic of grace.

What David really means when he says "I shall not be in want" is that we shall not lack the care and supervision of the good Shepherd. Everything God sees that we need, he will supply. The main thought is that we will not lack for proper care and attention. There will be no deficiency in the way the Shepherd looks after the sheep.

One of the best-known writers on Psalm 23 is Philip Keller, a man who for many years had first-hand experience of shepherding on sheep ranches in East Africa. He writes with great passion and insight about the pride that a shepherd takes in his flock, for the sheep are a reflection of the one who looks after them. He speaks with some disgust of a neighboring tenant shepherd who seemed to care little for his flock. They were always weak and thin, riddled with disease and parasites. Left to forage for themselves, they became prey to wild animals. Often they lacked food and shelter. Muddy water was all they had to drink. Meanwhile the tenant shepherd remained indifferent to their needs, callous to their plight.

How different this is from the care that the good Shepherd gives, and of which we can be certain. Keller describes him in this way:

> He is the owner who delights in his flock. For him there is no greater reward, no deeper satisfaction, than that of seeing his sheep contented, well fed, safe and flourishing under his care. This is indeed his very 'life'. He gives all he has to it. He literally lays himself out for those who are his. He will go to no end of trouble and labor to supply them with the finest grazing, the richest pasturage, ample winter feed, and clean water. He will spare himself no pains to provide shelter from storms, protection from ruthless enemies and the diseases and parasites to which sheep are so susceptible.[1]

What all this means is that we shall not lack the expert care and tender supervision of the good Shepherd. This is the key thought as the psalm begins, and everything else flows out of this wonderful relationship between Shepherd and sheep.

Testimony to the Shepherd's care can be found throughout scripture. It is a thought repeated by David himself in

Psalm 34, a song written after his deliverance from a scary moment at the hands of a Philistine king. "Fear the Lord, you his saints, for those who fear him lack nothing. The lions may grow weak and hungry, but those who seek the Lord lack no good thing" (34:9–10). It is a blanket assurance that he speaks of here, in the promise that we shall lack "no good thing." As we have already noted, it is God who determines and defines what is good, but that which is good will not be lacking in our lives.

Other testimonies are more specific. We saw earlier that the period of wandering in the desert was, for Israel, a time of being shepherded by God. During the long wilderness years, he continued to provide for them very tangibly, often in supernatural ways. Their experience continued to be a source of encouragement to God's people throughout the generations. Even by the time of Nehemiah, it was still being sung about: "For forty years you sustained them in the desert; they lacked nothing, their clothes did not wear out nor did their feet become swollen" (Nehemiah 9:21; compare Deuteronomy 2:7). What amazing provision, and what tangible expression of God's ability to care for his people!

The disciples of Jesus had a similar story to tell. Having left everything to follow him, they saw how God could provide for their needs even though they had no way of earning a living. To help them see the significance of this, and to underline the lesson for future occasions, Jesus asked them directly, "When I sent you without purse, bag or sandals, did you lack anything?" Their reply was just as clear and certain. "Nothing," they answered (Luke 22:35).

Material provision goes hand in hand with spiritual provision, and the apostle Paul was always keen to help believers realize that God has provided everything we need through his Son Jesus. The church at Corinth was perhaps one of the weakest of the New Testament churches. There were many problems within the congregation and much room for im-provement, yet in writing to them Paul does not shrink from giving thanks for them or reminding them of their spiritual resources in Christ: "For in him you have been enriched in every way—in all your speaking and in all your knowledge—because our testimony about Christ was confirmed in you. Therefore you do not lack any spiritual gift" (1 Corinthians 1:5–7). This poor, struggling congregation could be sure that they had everything they needed to make an impact on the pagan environment in which they lived. They could rely upon the sufficiency of God's provision for them. They already had every spiritual gift they needed to live effectively in such a hostile place.

It is this thought of the sufficiency of God's provision for us that most strikes me as I meditate on these words of David. God in his grace has guaranteed that we have all that we need in order to live for him. It reminds me of Peter's declaration: "His divine power has given us every-thing we need for life and godliness through our knowl-edge of him" (2 Peter 1:3). This is how I see the outworking of David's bold assertion. God continuously imparts to us the grace we need, to live lives that glorify him and impact our communities. Whenever we feel that we lack what it takes, we can confidently come to him and ask for what we need. He will never let us down. We flourish under his care.

Two things follow when we begin to live in the light of this gracious provision. First, we learn to be content. Many peo-ple we meet are discontented with their lot in life and they grumble and complain their way through each day, con-scious only of what they don't have. Those who live in a close relationship with the good Shepherd have a different out-look. They are more conscious of what they do have, rather than what they do not have. They are aware of what he has given them, and they are grateful. They are satisfied in him and with his provision for them. They are learning, with Paul, the secret of contentment (Philippians 4:11–13), and thus they are not in want.

Second, we are able to live with a freedom from care. Not that this is easy, for it seems so natural to worry and fret over the silliest things, but as we grow closer to the Shepherd and learn to trust him more, we are increasingly released from being over-concerned about our problems and difficulties. Sheep have a wonderful ability to live in the present moment, oblivious to anxiety about their futures. They take no thought for themselves. Rather, they let the shepherd do the worrying. Unfortunately, we are not so simple. Yet faith requires a childlike trust, and a growing confidence in the Shepherd's ability and willingness to care for us will lead us gradually to more carefree living.

For some years I pastored a church in the coal-mining area of Yorkshire. During the miners' strike in the mid 1980s, several of the men in the church were off work without pay for many months.

It was amazing how God provided for their needs during this desperate period. It was a hard time, but one during which we saw together the faithfulness of God.

One of the men, Bob, became so short of money at one point during the strike that he could not pay his electricity bill. Feeling somewhat downhearted and ashamed, he set off to the payment center to inform them that he had no money and could not pay. He was expecting his electricity to be cut off, and, with young children to care for, he wondered how they would cope. As he was walking down the street, another church member pulled up in his car, opened the window and passed him an envelope. "Hi Bob," he said. "When I was praying this morning I felt the Lord tell me to give you this." Then he drove off. When Bob opened the envelope, to his amazement, there was the exact amount he needed to pay the bill.

It wasn't only in financial ways that God met the needs of this group of men. They began to meet regularly for prayer and Bible study, and as they brought their needs to God and gave themselves to getting to know their faith better, they began to grow spiritually and to mature as people. They were able to cope with the pressure they were under, and to remain joyful and positive at a time of great stress for everyone. Physically, emotionally, and spiritually they found themselves cared for. Several eventually grew into leadership roles, and even now they look back on the period of the strike as one of great blessing. Why? Because God made sure they had everything they needed.

Experiences like this enable us to make with David this bold assertion: "The Lord is my Shepherd, I shall not be in want." The logic of grace tells us that if the first part is true, then so is the second. He is everything we need, and he will supply all that we need. This is what it means to have a living relationship with a living Shepherd.

Questions for Reflection

For individuals

1. Think back over your relationship with God. When did it become personal for you? What events led up to your being able to say, "The Lord is my shepherd"?

2. Consider the characteristics of a good shepherd. Which appeal to you the most?

3. "How we think about God determines how we relate to him." How do you normally relate to God? How might a deeper understanding of the fact that God is a shepherd help you to relate to him more easily?

4. In what ways do you see your own behavior like that of a sheep? Why do you need a shepherd?

5. What do you think it means to relate to God on the basis of grace, rather than on the basis of law or self-effort? How do you relate to him?

6. How have you personally seen the good Shepherd supply your needs?

For groups

1. With what people and events in your own lives do you associate Psalm 23?

2. Ask a few members of the group to share how they came to be able to say "The Lord is my shepherd."

3. What are the main characteristics of a good shepherd? How are these seen in Jesus?

4. Why do you think self-awareness is important in relationships? In what ways are people like sheep? Do you identify with any of these?

5. Why is it said that the shepherd–sheep relationship is one of grace? What does it mean to relate to God on the basis of grace?

6. What kind of needs has the good Shepherd promised to meet? Invite group members to share their personal experiences of this provision.

2
Learning to Rest

He makes me lie down in green pastures, he leads me beside quiet waters, he restores my soul. (vv. 2–3a)

❧

One of our greatest needs is to learn to rest. Caught up in the frenetic activity of a world that is getting faster all the time, our damaged souls cry out for the healing and refreshment that God alone can give.

7 Made to Lie Down

A priority for the shepherd is to lead his flock to where they can find pasture to eat and water to drink. Early in the morning he sets out, walking before them, and leading them to his chosen spot. Then, after spending the morning grazing, they are able to rest, lying down in the lush pasture that the shepherd has provided for them.

Nothing thrills a shepherd more than to see his flock rested and content. Sheep do not rest easily. If there is any sense of danger they will be on edge and are easily stampeded. Niggling flies and insects can trouble and disturb them, making them agitated. Sometimes there is friction between the sheep themselves as they jostle for position within the flock. And of course, if they are hungry or thirsty they will search around anxiously for grass to eat and water to drink. So, when the shepherd sees the flock lying down, he knows he has done a good job. They are being well cared for and are flourishing under his supervision. This gives him great delight.

It is interesting that this picture of restful contentment is the first description that David gives us of the work of the divine Shepherd, for "rest" is perhaps the main benefit of the gospel that Jesus came to bring. Sensing the heavy burden of religious rules and regulations under which many people lived, he proclaimed an alternative way of living and relating to God that was based on grace, not law. "Come to me, all you who are weary and burdened," he said, "and I will give you rest." Offering a liberating alternative, he gave this invitation: "Take my yoke upon you and learn from me, for I am gentle and humble in heart, and you will find rest for your souls. For my yoke is easy and my burden is light" (Matthew 11:28–30).

This need to find rest for our souls is one of our most basic needs, made all the more acute by the fast-paced world in which we live and the hectic lifestyles followed by many. We rush from one event to the next in a whirlwind of activity, with hardly a moment for ourselves or a chance to draw breath. E-mail and internet keep us continually informed and updated, while we remain constantly in touch with people through text messaging and cell phones. We fear to disengage from the world of activity in case we should fall behind in the race. We dare not slow down even for a second, such is the high-speed world in which we live. The result? Our souls are threadbare, our spirits exhausted, our bodies strained to the limit. We live on the edge of exhaustion, with tiredness a constant companion. Burnout is the price we pay, strained relationships part of the cost.

There is a better way to live, and the good Shepherd wants to make us lie down so that we can experience it. There is a strong sense of intentionality in the Hebrew expression used here. He doesn't exactly force us to lie down, but he highly recommends it! Concerned for our well-being, he knows that we need to learn how to rest. Our fast-paced society often forgets how to relax, and when we do take time to slow down, it is often accompanied by feelings of guilt.

How, then, does the good Shepherd help us to find a place of rest?

First, by offering us physical rest. Long ago in his wisdom God saw that it was not good for people to work ceaselessly without rest. He commanded that we should take the first day of the week as a sabbath, a day of rest from work and the demands of life (see Exodus 20:8–11). This follows his own pattern of work and then rest, and provides the basis for a healthy rhythm of life.

It has been pointed out that when God created the world he worked for six days and then rested on the seventh (the Sabbath). Man and woman were created on the sixth day (Genesis 1:27–31), which means that their first day in the world was a day of rest, a holiday (holy day). Thus God inscribed into our very beings not only the need for rest but also the legitimacy of rest and recreation, of relaxation and leisure. The divine order is to work from a place of rest. We have a tendency to reverse the order and work into rest— that is, to drive ourselves so hard that we eventually collapse in a heap and are forced to rest. No wonder we get sick so easily and feel out of sorts much of the time. The basic rhythm of life has been broken.

If we remember that holidays were originally holy days, we need not feel guilty when we do take time to rest. Indeed, when we keep the Sabbath (not in a legalistic sense of rules and regulations about what you can and can't do, but in the sense of taking time to worship, to rest and be renewed), we are doing something that God considers to be holy. He has blessed leisure and relaxation, and we are encouraged to build times for recreation into our busy schedules. Taking time out on a regular basis keeps us fresh, creative, and vibrant. It prevents us from becoming jaded and weary. We can give ourselves permission to rest because God intends that we do so.

Beyond physical rest, the good Shepherd has also provided for our spiritual rest, the inner peace that comes from knowing that our sins are forgiven and that we are in a right relationship with God. The reason he laid down his life for us was to deal once and for all with our sins. Now, because he has taken the punishment our sins deserved, we can be forgiven, cleansed, and justified—that is, placed into a new relationship with God and treated as if we had never sinned at all. The restless anxiety of a guilty conscience is stilled as we realize he has made atonement for us.

This new relationship with God is not of our own making. It is received as a gift of his grace, and because of that we no longer need to strive to make ourselves acceptable to him. We already are accepted, and simply need to grow into an awareness of how much we are loved by God, and how much he wants to do for us. Thus we are freed from trying in our own strength to make ourselves acceptable to God. We learn to rest in his grace and relax in the fact that we have now been reconciled to him.

What is more, the good Shepherd offers us emotional rest—the contentment that comes from knowing he has taken responsibility for our lives. Someone has said that this is the overwhelming need in our times. The rush of life, the pace of change, the pressures upon us, all combine to leave us emotionally drained. We desperately need help from beyond ourselves, to know that someone is watching out for us. We need someone to take the strain for us in our stressed-out lives. If it is true that the Lord is our Shepherd, then we ought to be able to live without the anxious care and fretful worry that so easily dominate our lives. Nothing calms a flock of sheep better than the presence of the shepherd. To know that God is with us is perhaps the best antidote to feelings of despair and worry. To concentrate through worship and scriptural meditation on the fact that our Shepherd is also the Lord enables us to hand over everything that frightens and disturbs us. The more our minds are focused on him, the greater the peace we have. Just to know he cares, and that he is with us, brings emotional healing and release.

So it is that our divine Shepherd brings us to a place of rest. We dare to lie down because he is in control, watching over our lives, thoughtful for our every concern. He leads us to the green pastures of his word so that we may feed ourselves upon the truths it contains and be secured again by the knowledge of his sovereign control of the world and our lives. He brings us to those quiet waters through the gentle ministry of the Holy Spirit, stilling our souls and filling us with assurance of his love. As we dare to linger in his presence, resting in his embrace, our souls are restored and we are healed.

I cannot read this part of Psalm 23 without thinking of the boy Samuel in the temple. It was his job to help the priest, Eli, with many mundane tasks, but he was a boy whose heart was open to God from an early age. At a time in Israel's history when things were at a low ebb spiritually, God chose to speak to Samuel one night as he lay asleep in the temple, near the ark of God. Being as yet unskilled in recognizing the voice of God, Samuel assumed that it was Eli calling him. The old man, annoyed at being woken from his sleep, assumed it was the boy's imagination.

When this had happened three times, Eli realized that it was God speaking to Samuel. His words of direction to the young lad are profound in their simplicity. He told the boy, "Go and lie down, and if he calls you, say, 'Speak, Lord, for your servant is listening'" (1 Samuel 3:1–10).

What is profound about these words is that they describe for us what it means to live for God from a place of rest. Eli advises the boy to go and lie down—in other words, to go back to sleep. Samuel doesn't need to stay awake all night, nervously waiting for God to speak. There is no need to pace up and down anxiously listening for the slightest sound, in case he might miss God's call. No, he can lie down and rest because God is quite capable of making himself heard. The initiative is with God. In his time he will speak, and he will speak clearly and loudly enough for Samuel to hear. When he does speak, Samuel is merely to respond with the open-hearted obedience of a servant, ready to do what the master requires. It is the submissive attitude of his heart that is important.

In this grace relationship with God that is at the heart of the Christian life, we too can learn to relax—to lie down, as it were, and let God take the initiative. He is well able to make the first move, and he is not dependent upon us. Trying too hard is one of the most common pitfalls in Christian living, for we forget that God is to be the prime mover, and our role is to respond, not initiate. It is the reason so many believers become exhausted in their attempts to serve God. Our conscientiousness and sense of responsibility can seem like Christian virtues, but often they obstruct the true flow of grace in our lives, substituting human effort instead of divine life. We never see the same economy of effort or fruitfulness of effect as when God moves and we simply respond in obedience. When that happens, the work is easy, natural, flowing, productive. When it originates within ourselves, it is often strained, difficult, exhausting, producing little. It is far better to take time to wait on God, to hear what he is saying, and then, to do what he says. This is the way of grace.

Sheep have only one responsibility—to listen to the shepherd's voice. Then, when he calls them out and goes on ahead of them, they follow trustingly. It is not difficult or onerous. In fact, it is easy, really—a picture of the way Jesus intended us to live.

8 Green Pastures

Thomas Kelly was a Quaker who lived in America in the first part of the twentieth century. Although he died at a fairly young age, his writings have helped many outside the boundaries of his own denomination to value stillness and silence. In particular, his little book *A Testament of Devotion* has introduced a more contemplative approach to many Christian activists.

It is in that book that he speaks of finding the "Divine Center," a place within ourselves where we are at rest and "the soul is at home with God." It enables us to live life beyond the fevered strain that characterizes so much of our contemporary experience. Interestingly enough, Kelly makes several references to Psalm 23 in this connection, linking the longing that many feel for a more God-centered life with the promises given in these verses. He urges us to recognize and respond to the longing of our own hearts for this kind of rest. "It is the Eternal Goodness calling you to return Home, to feed upon the green pastures and walk beside the still waters and live in the peace of the Shepherd's presence."[2]

The place to which the shepherd leads his flock is the place where they can find good pasture on which to graze. It is easy to forget that in the Middle East such pastureland is very scarce. Indeed, rich grasslands were often fought over by rival groups. If the shepherd knows where good pasture is to be found, it will be either because he knows the countryside very well and has searched it out, or because he has cleared the barren ground himself and tilled it until new grass appears. It is of primary concern to him that his flock has good pasture on which to feed. He wants the very best for them too, for he seeks green pasture—growth that is young, fresh, succulent.

We can be sure that the good Shepherd is equally concerned to provide the nourishment that our souls need. He is anxious to lead us to those places where we can feed the spiritual part of us, and find that centeredness of which Kelly speaks. And what is the pasture that he would give to us? It is nothing less than his very life imparted to us by his Spirit, the abundant life that Jesus promised: "I am the gate; whoever enters through me will be saved. He will come in and go out, and find pasture. The thief comes only to steal and kill and destroy; I have come that they may have life, and have it to the full" (John 10:9–10). Pasture is here equated with eternal life. The intention of Jesus is not to detract from our lives, but to add to them, to supply that which is missing. This he does by sharing his own life with us.

How, then, can we find this pasture for ourselves? Obviously it comes to us first and foremost through the living relationship we have with Jesus. But what are the sources of that life in practical terms?

Primarily, we find green pasture in the scriptures. The Bible is the main source of spiritual nourishment, not in and of itself, but because it speaks to us of Jesus. Simply reading it as an interesting book, or becoming familiar with the history it contains, will not help us particularly. We read it in order that we might find Jesus. The Pharisees made the mistake of becoming familiar with the scriptures intellectually, but missed the whole point of it. "You diligently study the scriptures," said Jesus, "because you think that by them you possess eternal life. These are the scriptures that testify about me, yet you refuse to come to me to have life" (John 5:39–40). The whole purpose of scripture is to bring us to Jesus, to show us all that he has done for us, and to reveal to us all that is ours in him.

From beginning to end, the Bible speaks of Jesus. Whether we read in the Old Testament or the New Testament, if we have eyes to see, we will find him and our faith will be built up. This was how the Master instructed the two disciples as they walked on the Emmaus road: "And beginning with Moses and all the Prophets, he explained to them what was said in all the scriptures concerning himself" (Luke 24:27). What a Bible study that must have been!

No wonder their hearts "burned within them" as he opened the scriptures to them. They were finding life, their souls were being nourished, their spirits set ablaze with love for him.

The reason there are so many malnourished Christians today is that so few take time to feed themselves upon God's word. The diet of many believers today consists only of second-hand tidbits from others at big events or celebrations. They do not know how to read the Bible for themselves, nor do they make time to do so. Selwyn Hughes, whose Bible reading notes are read worldwide, laments the decline of the quiet time—that period in the day set aside to meet with God in prayer and the reading of scripture.

One of the things that concerns me about many young Christians today is the fact that they are not taught to begin the day with God. Much of this, I know, is a reaction against the legalism that pervaded the Church a few decades ago. . . . Nowadays—generally speaking—we seem to have swung to the other extreme, regarding the daily Quiet Time as unimportant and irrelevant.[3]

There is a saying that you can lead a horse to water, but you cannot make it drink. We may amend this slightly and say, you can lead a sheep to pasture, but you can't make it graze. As one who preaches and teaches regularly, both in a local church and elsewhere, I am constantly staggered by the lack of lasting impact the Bible makes on people's lives. I do not believe for one moment that the fault lies with the Bible. I believe the reason so many are not transformed by what they read and hear is that they do not properly digest the word of God. It enters their minds, but not their hearts. They receive it gladly, but seldom apply it personally and directly.

If we are really to benefit from the Bible, we must learn to meditate on it. This is the process by which we chew over small portions of scripture until we not only understand their meaning but also see how they apply to our lives. It is the way by which the truth sinks down from our heads into our hearts, and nourishes our hungry souls. It is one of the most effective means by which we receive the life of God to invigorate our flagging spirits.

Author Ian Barclay tells the story of a minister who counseled a man referred to him by the local doctor. The man was president of a large American company, but lacked peace and direction in life. The minister gave him his own prescription. He ordered the man to read Psalm 23 five times a day for seven days, carefully, meditatively, and prayerfully, starting as soon as he woke in the morning. Immediately after breakfast he was to do the same thing, then also after lunch, then again after dinner, and finally as he went to bed. It was not to be a quick, hurried reading. He was to think about each phrase, giving his mind time to soak up as much of the meaning as possible. The minister promised the man that if he did this, at the end of one week things would be completely different for him.[4]

That minister understood the importance of meditation and the promise that goes with it: "Do not let this Book of the Law depart from your mouth; meditate on it day and night, so that you may be careful to do everything written in it. Then you will be prosperous and successful" (Joshua 1:8). Psalm 23, and the rest of the Bible, are the tender grass that God has provided for our spiritual sustenance. I am convinced that if more Christians took time to meditate on God's word like this, they would be stronger, happier, more Christlike, and more effective.

Meditation does not stand alone, however. At the same time as we take in the word of God, we need the Holy Spirit to reveal its truth to us. We cannot understand spiritual truth unaided. Our minds are limited, and we need the Spirit to enlighten us. This is why Paul so often prayed for revelation, for himself and others. Writing to the church at Ephesus he says:

> I keep asking that the God of our Lord Jesus Christ, the glorious Father, may give you the Spirit of wisdom and revelation, so that you may know him better. I pray also that the eyes of your heart may be enlightened in order that you may know the hope to which he has called you, the riches of his glorious inheritance in the saints, and his incomparably great power for us who believe. (Ephesians 1:17–19)

The reality is that human reason alone cannot fathom such deep spiritual truth. Our minds have to be opened by the Spirit of God so that these great facts can become life-giving truth to us. We need the Spirit to give us wisdom and revelation, so not only do we meditate on scripture, but we constantly pray that God will open the scripture to us and give us understanding. This is how the Shepherd leads us to green pasture, and how our souls are nourished.

Why do these green pastures become a place of rest? Because the scriptures tell me who I am, and all that I have in

Christ. They tell me what God is like, reminding me that he loves me, that he is in control of my life. They contain the promises that strengthen me in moments of doubt or fear. Above all, they point me to Jesus. As someone has said, "When by faith we are enabled to find rest in the promises, we are like sheep that lie down in the midst of the pasture."

9 Beside Quiet Waters

In his concern to take care of his flock as effectively as he is able, the shepherd leads them to where they have water to drink. Sheep need lots of water, and often find it on the dewy grass of early morning, but that is not enough. They need to drink from streams or pools, or have water provided for them from wells. Their instinctive fear of drowning means that they do not like to go near fast-flowing rivers or noisy brooks. If they are to drink, they prefer the gentle, quiet waters of which the psalmist speaks.

It is a characteristic of Eastern shepherds that they go ahead of their sheep, leading them from the front, rather than driving them from behind. This reminds us that the God of grace never forces or cajoles us to do his will. Rather he woos us with the voice of love, drawing us gently after him, leading in such a way that we are glad to follow. It is a style of leadership that many church leaders would do well to emulate.

The shepherd leads his flock to quiet waters. The expression "quiet waters" is translated in various ways—"waters of comfort," "still waters," "waters of rest" being just a few examples. One Hebrew scholar says that the word *menuhot* used here speaks of a state of rest where there is no strife and no fighting, no fear and no distrust. Theologian Marva J. Dawn, building on this insight, says, "Our shepherd Lord not only provides for our physical nourishment by taking us to green pastures, but also enfolds us in contentment and tranquility by leading us beside waters of stillness. Those words promise us profound solace for our spirits."[5]

Certainly the picture is one of a safe resting place, where the sheep are being refreshed. Water is so essential that it is universally a symbol of life, and in the Bible it generally speaks of the work of the Holy Spirit, who imparts to us the life of God. So what we have here is an illustration of the desire of God to refresh our souls by sharing his life with us. This he does by bringing us to a place of rest, to seasons of quietness and stillness.

Perhaps the greatest hindrance to our finding this place of rest is our compulsion to be busy. Because we are always on the move, and our lives are so full, we have little time simply to relax and enjoy God. It is this that prevents us from becoming "centered" in the way described by Thomas Kelly, whom we encountered at the start of the last chapter. Instead we live fractured and disintegrated lives, pulled in many directions at once, restless and agitated in our spirits. Our insistence on pleasing everyone, and our inability to say no to the demands placed on us (what Kelly calls our "frantic fidelity"), mean that we are overloaded and overstretched.

Although he wrote in 1941, Kelly's description of modern life resonates with us today.

> Even the necessary obligations which we feel we must meet grow overnight, like Jack's beanstalk, and before we know it we are bowed down with burdens, crushed under committees, strained, breathless, and hurried, panting through a never-ending program of

appointments. We are too busy to be good wives to our husbands, good homemakers, good companions of our children, good friends to our friends, and with no time at all to be friends with the friendless.[6]

It isn't surprising that in such a lifestyle, time for God is at a premium, and that leisurely periods of seeking God (so important for spiritual growth) are neglected. The result is that we become spiritually impoverished.

John Ortberg is an author and teaching pastor at Willow Creek Community Church in Barrington, Illinois. He tells how on one occasion he had called his spiritual director for advice, asking him what he should do to stay spiritually healthy. After a thoughtful pause his director replied, "You must ruthlessly eliminate all hurry from your life." Ortberg shares how this arrow of wisdom found its mark in his life, and he goes on to say, "For many of us the great danger is not that we will renounce our faith. It is that we will become so distracted and rushed and preoccupied that we will settle for a mediocre version of it."[7]

I wonder if you recognize the symptoms of an over-committed lifestyle in yourself?

Concerned for our well-being, the good Shepherd wants to lead us gently to resting places, to find pools of silence and tranquility in the rush and hurry of daily life, so that we can become integrated and whole again. His desire is to re-center us, to bring us back to the place where we have time to stop and drink of the living water he so freely gives.

Although the contemplative tradition in the church has long stressed the need for stillness and quiet, the evangelical and charismatic streams have tended toward a more active spirituality. However, many are now discovering for themselves the healthy balance that comes from deliberately integrating into their schedules periods set aside for quiet waiting upon God. The great biblical injunction "Be still, and know that I am God" (Psalm 46:10) is being seen in a new light, and many are beginning to learn how to put it into practice. They are allowing themselves to be led to the quiet waters, the waters of stillness.

When we are used to living at a fast pace, it is not easy to slow down, let alone stop. At first it feels unnatural and strange, and of course feelings of guilt at "doing nothing" quickly surface. If we can bear in mind that it is God who is calling us to slow down, and if we will persevere, we shall soon become familiar with a different rhythm, and the benefits of intentional times of stillness will gradually become evident in our lives.

Waiting on God is perhaps a lost art, but even a cursory glance at the Psalms will show how fundamental it is to a living relationship with God (see, for example, Psalms 27:14; 130:5–6). When we wait on God, we spend time with him in a leisurely way, enjoying his presence, reflecting on his love for us, delighting in his friendship. We may take time to worship or to meditate, and we may be alone or with others. We may pray with words or with silent prayer; we might write down our feelings or journal what we hear God saying to us. In the stillness we learn just to be, bringing ourselves as we are before a God who loves us as we are. We allow ourselves to live in the grace of God, and grace inevitably leads us to a place of intimacy and rest, sheltered in his healing presence. This is how God imparts his life to us, how he refreshes our souls. Whatever shape it takes, the point is that we are giving quality time to building our relationship with God.

For most of my adult life I have been involved in "full-time" Christian ministry, and I have worked hard and enthusiastically. I am by nature an activist, and until the last few years had no understanding or comprehension of the benefits of a more contemplative approach. Over the last few years, however, the good Shepherd has been gently drawing me to explore this area, and I have discovered a whole new way of relating to God. Once I overcame my initial fears about how I would cope with stillness and solitude, I have found that God has been able to show me more of his love for me, and draw me closer to him, simply through spending uninterrupted time with him. I have realized the importance of quiet days set aside to seek God, and of longer periods of retreat where I can come before God with no other agenda than to know him better. As a result I feel more integrated as a person, more at peace, and more centered on God.

It is not only those in Christian ministry who can benefit from making time to be still before God. Busy moms need space like this; so do those who care for others. Anyone whose life is busy and demanding needs to practice soul care, and give themselves the opportunity to be spiritually refreshed. It is not a luxury; it is a necessity. It won't just happen by itself, however: we have to be proactive and intentional, marking time out to look after our inner life and to develop our walk with God.

To those who live in the fast lane, American writer David Kundtz recommends the practice of *stopping*, which he says is learning how to be still even when you have to keep going. He talks about utilizing the "still points" that occur naturally in the midst of each day, as well as planning longer periods of "stopover" and, if possible, an occasional extended period or "grinding halt." His definition of stopping is interesting. "Stopping," he says, "is doing nothing as much as possible for a definite period of time (one second to a month) for the purpose of becoming more fully awake and remembering who you are."[8]

I like that definition very much, and I think it can easily be applied to the times when the good Shepherd leads us beside the quiet waters, to spiritual resting places. There we learn to do nothing other than to be with him. There we become more fully awake to who he is and the care he takes over us. There we remember who we are, his beloved ones, the sheep of his pasture, bought at a great price. And whether for a moment or a day, deliberately stopping to have time with God will always result in time well spent.

10 Restoring My Soul

Under normal circumstances, sheep that are well fed and watered will thrive, and the picture that David paints for us here is one of an exceptionally contented flock, lying down in the lush green pastures, resting by the quiet waters. It is an idyllic scene, and one for which the shepherd strives. Yet the reality is that, even with the best of care, there will be sheep that are in need of help.

Some sheep will wander away and injure themselves by falling or getting trapped in thorny bushes. Others may be wounded by predators, or preyed upon by wild animals. A few will get diseased and become sick. This means that the shepherd must always keep a watchful eye over his flock, and be alert for the individual sheep that need his help. Indeed, it is this careful, patient tending of the flock that characterizes a good and skillful shepherd. He is there to strengthen the weak, to heal the sick, and to bind up the injured.

To restore something means to return it to its original condition, to put it back in working order. It means to bring back to health, to mend something that is broken. The expression "he restores my soul" suggests that the good Shepherd is concerned to watch over the health of his flock, and to nurse us back to recovery. Under normal circumstances we can expect that if we stay close to the Lord, feed on his word, and regularly spend time with him, we will continue to be spiritually healthy. But we all know that life is not that simple, and sometimes, even though we have a good Shepherd watching over us, we too find ourselves bruised and hurting, sick and unwell. That is when we need him to restore our souls.

The restoration of our souls is something worthy of our attention. The very expression suggests that things can go wrong with our souls, that they can be damaged or spoiled in some way. It implies that we are sometimes vulnerable, open to attack, prone to injury. It also signifies that we can get the care and attention that we need, that no situation is hopeless, that we can be brought back to normal again.

Shepherds speak about a sheep being "cast"—that is, when it falls over and cannot get back on its feet again. This is a common condition among sheep, especially those heavy with young, and is the origin of the phrase "to be cast down." If a shepherd finds a sheep in such a state, he must gently lift it up and help it to its feet.

This reminds us of the biblical injunction of Galatians 6:1: "Brothers, if someone is caught in a sin, you who are spiritual should restore him gently." Sometimes, sadly, we do find ourselves defeated by sin. We fail to live up to our own high standards, and fall in some particular way. Does that mean we are finished? Does it mean we can no longer walk with God? No, for the Bible also says that where sin abounds, grace abounds even more (Romans 5:20). There is free and full forgiveness available to us, and as we repent and turn from our sin, we are restored into fellowship with God.

David himself knew this from first-hand experience, and he also knew the effect that sin had on his soul. Following his adultery with Bathsheba, and his complicity in the murder of her husband, Uriah, he lost all joy and peace. Eventually he cried to God in repentance, seeking forgiveness, and asking God in his mercy, "Restore to me the joy of your salvation" (Psalm 51:12). We can assume from what he says in Psalm 23:3 that God heard his prayer and that his fractured, tortured soul found restoration and recovery through the wonderful grace of God.

This means that there is always a way back. Whatever mistakes we have made, however great our failure, we can be both forgiven and restored. This is the wonder of the mercy of God, the marvel of his grace. He goes on forgiving us, time and time again. Does it mean that we take advantage of his grace? Not at all. In fact, the free forgiveness and mercy of God has the opposite effect. It makes us more grateful, more determined to please him, more unwilling to let him down again. According to Jesus, those who have been forgiven much love much (Luke 7:47).

There is another restoration of soul that we need—the kind that comes when we are spiritually and emotionally drained through giving out to others. Christian workers can sometimes forget their own needs in their desire to serve others, and they may fail to care for their own souls. Anyone who is concerned to help others is vulnerable in this area. We give and give until there is nothing more to give. Our souls shrivel up within us, we lose our creativity, and our zest for life disappears. The well inside us becomes empty.

Even Jesus was aware that when he ministered to others, virtue went out from him (Luke 6:19; 8:46). This was why he was careful to take time to be alone often with his Father so that he might be renewed and refreshed himself. It is the answer to our own need too. Time alone with God, lingering in his presence, waiting upon him, is one of the surest ways to the restoration of soul that we so badly need.

Elijah suffered this form of spiritual burn-out. Stressed and strained from his encounter with Jezebel and the priests of Baal, he ran away into the desert, lonely and afraid. Depression and self-pity swept over him. He felt totally alone, deserted and exhausted. Suicidal thoughts swirled around in his mind. The good Shepherd was watching over him, however, and came to tend this wounded sheep. First an angel appeared and ministered to his physical need. Then the Lord himself came, speaking not in the terrifying loudness of earthquake, wind, or fire, but in the gentle whisper of love. It was all Elijah could cope with, but it was just what he needed. Refreshed and restored, he was ready once more to do what he had to do (see 1 Kings 19).

Psychiatrist Dr. Marjory Foyle has spoken of those who are "honorably wounded" in the service of God. There are many such people who have given themselves unstintingly to spreading the gospel and to caring for the poor and needy. There is no shame in admitting that we are exhausted and at the point of collapse. It is better to seek the help that we need from the gracious Shepherd, as well as from the hands of the "angels" (skilled, caring professionals) he sends to care for us. However low we may have sunk, his hand is always able to lift us up again. Those who hope in the Lord will renew their strength (Isaiah 40:31).

A letter that I received recently reminds me that there is yet one more group of people who need their souls to be restored. It is those who find themselves bruised and hurt within the church, wounded inadvertently by friendly fire. The letter was from a woman who had attended a training course I led. She wrote as a way of expressing the pain and hurt she was feeling, a form of therapy for her. In her letter she said that after forty years as a Christian she could no longer continue in the institutional church. She and her husband had both been so battered and bruised that there was no way they could remain, even though they both still firmly believe in God and continue to be committed to knowing Christ. I felt extremely sad as I read what she had to say.

If this were an isolated case it would still be tragic, but the truth is that I know many people who have had a similar experience, and for whom church has been anything but a positive experience—leaders hurt by church members, and church members wounded by leaders.[9] It is a common story. Whatever happened to church as a community of grace? Perhaps a fundamental reason for the lack of love within congregations is that we have taken our eyes off the good Shepherd. Our obsession with numerical growth has resulted in churches that are driven rather than relaxed. It is not surprising that when our vision ceases to be Jesus, and is replaced by something else, we turn on each other. If we are out of love with him, it is not surprising that we are out of love with each other. Sheep that are stressed, apparently, have a tendency to bully one another. It seems to be a trait shared by some Christians.

Even for those who have been hurt by the church, however, there is hope. They too can be lovingly restored by the gentle Shepherd. It takes time, and is a slow and gradual process. Once trust has been broken, it is hard to mend, but it can be mended. My own church congregation has sought to be a community built upon grace. It is challenging, and not at all easy to live out that ambition in the reality of human relationships, but it is happening. In our fellowship there are several who have recovered from damaging experiences of church, and who are learning to trust again, and to give themselves freely once more.

Whether it be from the hurts caused by our own folly, the pain of finding ourselves over-stretched, or the wounds of friendly fire, there is a restoration of the soul that can take place as we turn once more to the good Shepherd. He alone is the one who can help us. Only he loves us without condition and without reservation. He understands us fully and accepts us as we are, loving us back to wholeness, helping us to find rest for our souls again.

Shopping in our local town one day, my wife and I entered a well-known department store for a coffee. As we drank, Evelyn pointed out to me the words that were written on the inside of the mug I was drinking from: "Relax! Refresh! Revive!"

These words seem to sum up what David is saying in this section of Psalm 23.

Relax! God wants us to learn to lie down, to take time to rest physically, allowing ourselves to "chill out" before God. We can rest in his acceptance of us and in the security of the relationship we have with him—safe, because it is based on his grace, not our efforts; and at peace, because he has taken hold of our lives and will never let go even for an instant.

Refresh! We can be refreshed through his word and by the ministry of the Holy Spirit as we wait upon God. As we open up our hearts to him, he will speak to us, feeding our souls, and as we quietly worship him, his Spirit will minister to our innermost beings, touching our spirits and releasing his life within us.

Revive! The outcome will be that because we have been rested and refreshed, our souls will be restored. Gradually, we will regain our strength in God. Slowly confidence will return, and we will even find ourselves ready again for the battle, fit once more to take our place on the frontline of service for God.

Questions for Reflection

For individuals

1. How would you describe your lifestyle in the light of this section of the book? Do you feel the need for rest? If so, what kind of rest? Physical? Spiritual? Emotional?

2. Why do you think grace brings us to a place of rest? How might this benefit you?

3. What does it mean to live from a "Divine Center"? How can the scriptures help us with this?

4. Do you share the compulsion to be busy? If so, why? How can you bring more stillness into your life?

5. Do you identify with the need for restoration of soul? In what way? From failure? From exhaustion? From friendly fire?

For groups

1. Do you agree that one of our greatest needs is to learn to rest? If so, why?

2. Identify the three kinds of rest that the good Shepherd offers. Discuss each of them in turn, thinking about their personal relevance.

3. What do you understand by the term "Divine Center"?

4. Discuss the idea of a regular Quiet Time. Is it a helpful practice or not? What makes it work? What makes it difficult?

5. Do you share the compulsion to be busy? Why are so many people so very busy? Is it possible to eliminate hurry from our lives? What would be the benefits?

6. What are the three types of restoration mentioned in chapter 10? Invite the group to share personal experiences of any of these.

PART **3**

Learning to Trust

He guides me in paths of righteousness for his name's sake. Even though I walk through the valley of the shadow of death, I will fear no evil, for you are with me; your rod and your staff, they comfort me. (vv. 3–4)

❧

Trust is at the heart of any relationship. It is something that grows, as we experience the faithfulness of the one in whom we place our trust. The Good Shepherd calls us to follow him and, in all the changing circumstances of life, to learn to put our trust in him.

11 He Guides Me

A wise shepherd knows the importance of keeping his flock on the move. Left to themselves, sheep will eat the pasture until there is nothing left and the ground is left bare and barren. In order to avoid over-grazing the land, they have to be carefully guided by their shepherd into fresh pastures. The longer the shepherd is with them, the more they come to trust him. They recognize him and know his voice. When the time comes to move on, and he calls to them, they willingly follow behind.

Jesus made reference to this when he spoke of himself as the good Shepherd. "He calls his own sheep by name and leads them out. When he has brought out all his own, he goes on ahead of them, and his sheep follow him because they know his voice" (John 10:3–4). Later he reemphasizes this same trusting relationship. "My sheep listen to my voice; I know them, and they follow me" (John 10:27). It seems from this that sheep are easily led. If the shepherd calls, they follow, for they have an instinctive trust in him. From past experience they know that he has always provided for them, so in simple trust they move with him. He has won their confidence.

The Christian life, at its heart, is a life of following Jesus. The very first invitation that he gives is the call to "Come, follow me" (Mark 1:17; 2:14). As we set out on the path of discipleship, the same call comes repeatedly, urging us on in our obedience to the Shepherd's voice. In moments of hesitancy or uncertainty, he calls again, reminding us, as he did Peter, that he wants us to follow in his steps (John 21:19; 1 Peter 2:21). He has plans and purposes for us, inviting us into the adventure of a life that is led by him. Confidently he goes ahead of us, leading by example, drawing us gently after himself.

We should not underestimate the radical nature of this call to discipleship. It is not that we are inviting him to share the journey with us as a kind of adviser or helpful associate. Rather, he is inviting us to share the journey with him. He is asking that we hand over control to him, that we give up our own plans and begin to share his. He wants us to allow him to map out the way ahead, regardless of where it may take us and how challenging it might be. He asks us to hand over the steering wheel to him, to surrender our right to self-determination. It is a big request, for we human beings have minds and wills of our own, and we are not so easily led as sheep.

This is why the question of surrender to God soon arises in the lives of those who truly want to be his disciples. Some issue will quickly emerge where our initial decision to follow him will be tested, and we will have to choose between our own will and the will of God. No area of life is to be left outside of his control. Any major decision has to be made in the light of his will—the career we choose, our choice of life partner, where we live, what we do with our time and money, how we serve, our attitude to possessions, and so on. Nothing is excluded from his takeover bid. How completely we yield to his claims upon us will determine how much he is able to use us in coming days. The more surrendered we are, the more his Spirit is able to work in and through us. The more co-operative we are, the more we will enjoy the peace and joy that comes from a heart that is fully obedient.

We need to understand that the good Shepherd never forces his will upon us, nor does he seek a reluctant, grudging capitulation. He looks for the response of love, the happy yielding of someone who gives themselves unreservedly to the lover of their soul. He is prepared to wait, too, for that moment of glad surrender, carefully wooing us to himself through his goodness, drawing us by his grace. The more we understand of what he has done for us, the deeper our grasp of his Calvary love, the easier it is to give ourselves back to him. We love because he first loved us (1 John 4:19).

In the midst of all this, it is important that we are learning to trust God. Trust comes with the experience of relating to someone else. The more we find them to be faithful and reliable, the easier it is to trust them. Our ability to trust grows and is enlarged with each new experience of the dependability of the other person. Every new experience we have of the faithfulness of God encourages us to trust him with more of our lives. Each time the good Shepherd demonstrates again that he is capable and competent to lead us, the seed of faith grows within us, and we are enabled to trust him more. We cannot make ourselves trust. It is the byproduct of experiencing consistent reliability.

For some people, trust does not come easily. Perhaps their life experience has made them wary of trusting anyone. Children who have been abandoned by parents often find it difficult to establish trusting relationships in later life. Those who have been let down badly by another person—say, within a marriage relationship—can also be hesitant to risk giving themselves again to someone else. Such painful experiences with people can mean that some find it difficult to trust God. The only answer is to remember that we are talking here about a good Shepherd, one who is utterly reliable and completely worthy of trust. He will never let us down, never take advantage of us, never walk out on us. The mistrust that we feel in our hearts can be healed, and we can learn to trust again, but it may not be easy. Only if we are willing to take the first few hesitant steps in trusting him will we discover his total trustworthiness. We must not allow fear to hold us back.

And where does the Shepherd lead us? In paths of righteousness, or, more simply put, "in right paths." He knows exactly what is good for us, and where he wants to take us. We can trust him to guide us because he has our best interests at heart. "For I know the plans I have for you," declares the Lord, "plans to prosper you and not to harm you, plans to give you hope and a future" (Jeremiah 29:11). Strengthened by the promise of this verse, countless believers have dared to trust God with their lives, and to believe that he is worthy of their trust. Stepping out in faith, they have responded to his call and found him to be true to his word.

One of my own early experiences of being led by God came when my wife and I went to serve in Sarawak, on the island of Borneo. It was my first time abroad, apart from a brief school holiday to Belgium, when I had been quite homesick, so I was a little apprehensive about such a major uprooting. Nevertheless, the sense of being "called" was so great that we responded and, in 1975, found ourselves doing language study in the small coastal town of Miri.

As part of our orientation program, we went on a trek into the jungle and stayed in a longhouse about three days' journey upriver from the coast. One late afternoon we went to bathe in the river—quite a new experience in itself for us, but part of the daily pattern of life in that culture. As I lay there, surrounded by rugged mountains and dense tropical rainforest, with the cool waters swirling around me, I experienced a sudden and profound sense of peace and well-being, of being at home. "This is great," I thought to myself.

"I really feel I belong here." It seemed strange that I had felt lost and bewildered in Belgium, yet was at home and relaxed in Borneo, but I had an amazing sense in that moment that I had been made for this place, that I fit. The subsequent years proved this to be true. We enjoyed eight exciting and fruitful years in that beautiful land with its lovely people. It became our home in every sense and still holds a major part in our affections. God knew it was the right place for us, and that early experience of his leading provided a platform of trust for us in future responses to God's leading.

As well as guiding us in ways that are right for us, he also leads in ways that are consistent with his own character. This is one way of understanding the expression "for his name's sake." "Paths of righteousness" then refers to the fact that he only ever moves us to do things that are in line with his own righteous nature. He will never ask us to do anything that is unholy, immoral, or impure. Neither does he lead us to do things that are cruel, unjust, or oppressive of others. He will not ask us to lie or cheat. These things would be inconsistent with who he is, and would bring shame upon him. This is one of the ways in which we can verify that we are being led by God. We can ask the question, "Does this glorify God? Is it consistent with his character? Does it uphold his name?"

So, when I was confronted with a particular situation on an overseas trip, I was able to discern God's will quite clearly. Someone shared with me that her husband had taken another woman and felt that God was telling him that she was to become his second wife. Knowing that God only ever leads us in paths of righteousness, it was easy to see that this was not God's will. He would not lead a man to betray his wife and be unfaithful to her. He would never ask someone to break their marriage vows. This man was clearly self-deceived, doing what so many people do—making the "will of God" suit their own selfish desires.

How, then, does the good Shepherd actually lead us? By speaking to us and enabling us to recognize his voice. This is primarily the work of the Holy Spirit, and is a distinguishing mark of all true believers. We have an intuitive awareness that God is speaking to us. We can recognize his voice. As Paul said, "those who are led by the Spirit of God are sons of God" (Romans 8:14). The whole exciting story of the book of Acts is the story of men and women who recognized the voice of God and responded to his leading.

Scripture provides a second and standard way by which God guides us. The Bible contains the basic principles of conduct that become normative for us in daily life. In addition, the Holy Spirit sometimes highlights particular passages or verses to us in a personal way, applying them to our particular circumstances and needs. It is amazing how a word or phrase can suddenly leap off the page at us, shedding light on our path and bringing clarity of purpose to us.

Circumstances themselves are another way by which we are guided. Generally speaking, if something is God's will, then things work together for us in that direction, and we find what is sometimes called an open door. On the other hand, if something is not God's will for us, we cannot make it happen; the door remains firmly closed (see Revelation 3:7). Other ways by which God may speak to us include words of prophecy and, less frequently, dreams and visions. For myself, I feel it is always important to share major decisions about guidance with trusted friends and spiritual advisers. We all have the capacity to deceive ourselves, and a wise person looks to others to confirm or deny the validity of what they sense is the voice of God. As Proverbs says, "Make plans by seeking advice" (20:18).

The responsibility in guidance is always with God. He is committed to leading us and therefore to speaking to us. Our responsibility is to hear his voice and to respond in obedience. We are to trust that he knows what is best for us and that he will lead us safely along the path he has marked out for us. As he reveals his will to us, he gives us the grace to follow, working in us all that we need both to delight in that will and also to carry it out (Philippians 2:12–13). The Christian life then becomes an exciting adventure in discovering and doing the will of God.

12 The Valley of Deepest Darkness

In leading his flock onwards in search of fresh pasture, the shepherd must often choose to follow a path which, to the sheep, appears dark and forbidding. The way to better grass often involves being led into steep and treacherous ravines and valleys until, eventually, new pasture is reached. At such times, the sheep may feel afraid and vulnerable. Only the presence of the shepherd with them prevents them from panic.

Having established the first principle of discipleship as being that the sheep follow wherever the Shepherd leads them, the next principle is to realize that sometimes the Shepherd may choose to lead us into difficult and challenging places—in fact, into the "valley of the shadow of death" or the "valley of deepest darkness" as some translations describe it.

This is perhaps the best-known part of the psalm, and the reason that Psalm 23 has become so popular down the ages. Particularly at times of death and bereavement, people turn to these words for comfort and reassurance, for they identify with an experience that is common to all people, at all times, and in all cultures—the experience of suffering. They may not give any profound answers to the philosophical questions that surround the questions of pain and sorrow and the presence of evil in the world, but they do provide a way of coping with the distress we all feel from time to time.

We may well feel, when suffering comes our way, that we are outside the will of God, but no, the path of righteousness itself sometimes leads us into circumstances that are difficult, and where we are called upon to trust him more than ever before. Hard times do not necessarily mean that we have done something wrong or that we have displeased God in some way. Neither do they imply that God has left us or abandoned us. It is more likely to be part and parcel of following obediently, for God does not promise that the path before us will always be smooth and easy. Indeed, Jesus warned that the road that leads to life is narrow, and only a few are willing to walk it (Matthew 7:13–14).

The "valley experience" can describe almost any time when we feel lonely, afraid and vulnerable. It refers to those periods in life when we are baffled and perplexed, bruised and battered. Obviously it can refer to facing death or suffering bereavement, but it could be financial difficulties, the break-up of a marriage, serious illness, concerns over our children, business problems, issues at work, periods of doubt and uncertainty, despair and discouragement, strife within the church. The list is endless. What they all have in common is this—they challenge our faith in God and his goodness, and give the impression that evil is about to triumph.

It is just at this point that we are called upon to trust God, to believe that the good Shepherd knows what he is doing. It has been said that trust is faith in a dark place—the ability to keep on believing and hoping in God even when all seems lost. Nothing so purifies our faith as a period of trial. Why is it that we believe in God? Because of what he gives us, or for who he is? Only when the blessings are removed does the real nature of our faith become clear, both to ourselves and to others.

The story of Job asserts that Satan cannot believe that it is possible for human beings to love God simply for his own sake. As far as he is concerned, people believe in God only for what they can get out of him. Remove the tangible blessings, and they will soon stop believing. Why does Job believe? Because God has blessed his life. "Take away the blessings," says Satan, "and you will see that he doesn't believe any more" (see Job 1:9–11).

Thus Job's life becomes the focus of a spiritual battle as, one by one, the blessings are removed and he enters the valley of deepest darkness. Of course he has his moments of doubt, and he gets angry with God. Sometimes he is bewildered and confused, but amazingly his faith holds firm and he comes through his ordeal still trusting in God. His faith has been purified; it has been refined like gold.

It is not being over-dramatic to say that a similar struggle takes place in the life of anyone who seriously wants to follow God. The good Shepherd will deliberately lead us into difficult places so that our faith may be purified and matured. We will find ourselves exposed to severe trial and put under the greatest of temptations, all to develop trust within us and make us rely not on ourselves but on God.

Nothing so glorifies God as the continuing trust of a man or woman in him when walking through the valley of deepest darkness. Trust is the highest compliment we can give to anyone, and God is delighted when he sees that we trust him despite our doubts and fears. Author Brennan Manning has said, "It may mean more to Jesus when we say 'I trust you', than when we say 'I love you.'"[10] These are weighty words, worth pondering. It is easy to love God when things are going well and the blessings are in place, but much harder, and yet more authentic, to keep on loving him when the blessings have disappeared. Trust takes us deeper into love, beyond the shallow surface of first attraction, to the underlying belief in the fundamental goodness and reliability of the other. Valley experiences reveal whether or not we truly believe in the goodness and love of God.

Manning says that what we need at such times is a "ruthless trust." By ruthless he means "without pity," for he sees the greatest enemy of trust as being the self-pity that so easily envelops us when things are going against us. Of course there is a natural and understandable degree of feeling sorry for ourselves when we are in the midst of suffering and hardship. We would not want to minimize the pain and agony that others go through, or to over-simplify how they should respond in such circumstances. What Manning means is that we need to deal with the malignant and paralyzing self-pity that is always ready to overwhelm us and prevent us from continuing in steady obedience. At such moments we need a heroic faith, the courage to keep on believing and trusting despite our feelings and fears.

Such a response is possible only because the God of all comfort and the Father of mercies pours his sustaining grace into our lives. It is not by our own grit and determination that we can get by, but by the manifestation of God's power in our weakness. The apostle Paul, for example, struggled with what he called a "thorn in the flesh." Whatever the identification of this particular problem, it was clearly something painful and agonizing that he wanted rid of, but God chose rather to give him strength to endure. God spoke clearly to him a word of life-giving reassurance: "My grace is sufficient for you, for my power is made perfect in weakness" (2 Corinthians 12:7–10). That same grace is available to everyone who is called to walk through the valley of deep darkness. The God who calls us to follow him has promised to sustain us every step of the way.

This decisive movement into a deeper trust is what Manning calls a "second conversion," a movement of grace in our hearts that takes us from mistrust to trust. It is a conversion that must be renewed daily and every time we find ourselves once again in the dark valley, for there are many such valleys on our journey.

As we have seen so often, much of David's own personal experience lies behind the words of this great psalm. Despite being God's chosen king, and a man who loved God dearly, there had been many dark moments in his life. The shadow of death had fallen upon him. He had felt the pain of the loss of his closest friend, Jonathan, and had suffered the loss of his own dear son, Absalom. He had known the darkness of exile and the sting of betrayal. There had been times of bewilderment and despair, of failure and disgrace. Yet through it all, God had been with him, and he remained confident and assured for the days that lay ahead.

Discipleship is no easy option. It is not for the faint-hearted. It demands courage, even sometimes heroism, but it is abundantly worthwhile. The Shepherd knows what he is doing and is utterly trustworthy. If he leads us into the valley, he will certainly bring us out again, guiding us safely to the other side.

13 The Divine Companion

Sheep seem to have an instinctive awareness of the presence of their shepherd. If they can see him or hear the sound of his voice, they are secure and at peace. Without him they become anxious and nervous. When passing through dark and frightening places, it is essential, therefore, that they know he is with them. The shepherd does his best to let them know he is there, walking among them, calling out to them, and making himself both seen and heard.

What sustains us through the hard times in life? It is that same sense of the presence of the good Shepherd. It has been said that that presence is the antidote to fear, and certainly the conscious awareness that God is with us is essential if we are to cope with the feelings of anxiety and worry that threaten to engulf us in our moments of darkness. "For you are with me" is a certainty born out of David's own nightmare experiences of abandonment and betrayal, of humiliating flight and heart-stopping moments. It is a promise on which every trusting believer must learn to depend.

Many commentators draw attention to the change in pronouns at this point in the psalm. The more impersonal "he" suddenly becomes the more intimate "you," as if the thought of the valley and its difficulty reminds David of the closeness to God that can be experienced at such times. It is a strange thing, but adversity has its way of bringing us nearer to God and making us more aware of his presence. This is one of the main blessings of such moments, and helps us to understand a little of why God allows us to go through such experiences.

I know there are some for whom the valley of deep darkness means the loss of all conscious awareness of God. It involves what St. John of the Cross called the "dark night of the soul," when a person seems unable to apprehend God at all, even though they formerly experienced his presence constantly. They feel abandoned, aware only of dryness and emptiness and an aching hunger for God. Such experiences have been written about for centuries in the classics of spiritual literature, and some would say that such periods are part of a necessary passage in spiritual transformation, bringing us to the end of one phase of knowing God and opening up for us new ways of relating to him. They can perhaps be described as "the Easter Saturday of the soul," that time of waiting in the darkness between the end of one thing (the death of Good Friday) and the beginning of another (the resurrection of Easter Sunday).

For others, the darkness of the valley speaks of the depression and mental anguish that they experience almost continually. Life for them really is like passing through a valley of deep gloom from which there is little relief. All of us have periods of slight depression, but these are soon over. For a few people, the gloom never seems to lift. Ian Barclay, in *He Is Everything to Me*, devotes a whole chapter to this subject, citing many well-known Christians who have battled with depression. It is said that in Britain, for example, one out of every ten people will suffer from mental illness at some time in their life. It is inevitable, therefore, that some

Christians will face this particular form of darkness. By reason of their personality and make-up they seem more prone to depression.

While validating the reality of both the dark night of the soul and the darkness that is depression, it is important to say that neither is to be the norm. It is only our apprehension of God's presence that is affected in such seasons. Whether we are aware of it or not, God is still present with us, for it is impossible for him to abandon his people. The reason that Jesus experienced the horror of God-forsakenness on the cross was so that we might never know what it is to be abandoned by him. His agonized cry, "My God, my God, why have you forsaken me?" (Matthew 27:46), means that he endured that awful abandonment so that we do not have to. On a cloudy day, when we do not see the sun, we do not conclude that it has ceased to exist or stopped shining simply because we do not feel its presence. We know that, hidden from our eyes behind the clouds, the sun shines as brightly as ever. Likewise, faith dares to believe that even when there is no emotional awareness of God's presence, he is still with us, shining his love upon us in faithful consistency.

Sometimes unseen, often unfelt, the God who cannot abandon us is always close by. Though he may appear to hide himself for a time, in the end his presence will break forth into our lives again like the sun in the morning. And even when he seems far off, his gracious influence is still at work in our lives, sustaining and keeping us, imparting to us strength we never knew we had. The good Shepherd will never abandon his sheep. We learn to walk by faith, not by sight, and to trust in the reliability of his promise and the faithfulness of his character.

The promise of our shepherding God is that he will never leave us or forsake us. Through the prophet Isaiah he gave this assurance: "When you pass through the waters, I will be with you; and when you pass through the rivers, they will not sweep over you. When you walk through the fire, you will not be burned; the flames will not set you ablaze. For I am the Lord your God" (Isaiah 43:2–3). Whether we face floods or fires (or any other calamity in life), he is there to lead and guide us.

The writer to the Hebrews takes hold of a similar assurance to remind his readers of a promise first given to Israel as they entered the promised land. "Never will I leave you; never will I forsake you" (Hebrews 13:5). *The Message* translates this in its own punchy style as "I'll never let you down, never walk off and leave you." A more literal expression draws out the negatives in the original Greek that make it even more emphatic: "I will never leave you nor forsake you, not never, no-how." Trust involves taking hold of such promises as these, and hanging on to them until we are through the valley. We need to believe that God is as good as his word.

The greatest reassurance of all, however, comes through our awareness that, in Jesus, God has stepped into our world and lived our life. Far from abandoning us, he became one of us, entering our world of time and space, taking human form and experiencing its joys and its sorrows. He became Emmanuel, God with us. In sharing our humanity, he is able now to serve as a merciful and faithful high priest on our behalf, not only interceding for us but pouring his sustaining grace on our lives. We are not alone in the valley, for he comes to us again and again in our need as our Emmanuel, the ever-present helper in time of need.

This was Paul's experience. At one of the lowest points in his life, he felt that everyone had deserted him. Arrested and put on trial for his faith, no one came to help him; everyone abandoned him. "But the Lord stood at my side," he writes, "and gave me strength" (2 Timothy 4:16–17). Dark as his circumstances were, and bleak as his future must have looked, he found himself wrapped in the divine presence. The Shepherd was watching over him.

Nor was it the first time that the great apostle had needed to know the reassurance of the divine presence. It had happened years before in Corinth, when opposition to his preaching was strong, and inside he felt lonely and afraid. One night God spoke to him in a vision. "Do not be afraid; keep on speaking, do not be silent. For I am with you, and no one is going to attack and harm you, because I have many people in this city" (Acts 18:9–10). Just when he needed it most, reassurance came. In the darkness, light began to shine. Strengthened inside, he was able to continue his ministry and cope with its pressures.

Such supernatural occurrences are quite rare in my experience. Usually the presence of God is communicated to us in an inexplicable awareness of his nearness, an intuitive sense that he is there. It cannot be explained in rational terms; it is an intuitive knowledge beyond words, but real nonetheless. It may come in a sudden experience of peace, or in a deep-seated awareness of a quiet joy filling our hearts. Occasionally it is experienced as a simple knowledge that all is going to be well, or as the ability to relax in the midst of turmoil. God draws near to us and we feel his presence. Perhaps most often, though, it comes to us fleshed out in the love and concern of others, the spoken words and caring actions that remind us that God has not left us.

Dr. Leslie Weatherhead, the famous Methodist minister, was once called to visit a woman whose husband had died suddenly and tragically. Friends had gathered to comfort her and sat with her as she spoke to the minister. "Where's God in this?" she asked accusingly. Weatherhead thought for a moment, then pointed to one of the friends sitting close by with her arm around the woman. "I think he's there," he said quietly, "in the comfort of your friend."

Perhaps sometimes we take for granted the help and support that others give to us in our times of need, but we should recognize that, in their presence, God is also present. His love and care for us become tangible and real in the concern and thoughtful gestures of others. This also means, of course, that we can be the means of making his presence real to others by responding to the promptings of the Spirit to express his love in practical ways.

I have been amazed myself at how often a word of encouragement has come to me just when I needed it. During a low point for me a few weeks ago, I said to God, "Lord, I need some encouragement." I didn't pray with any great fervor, but I did mean it. That same morning a letter came from a woman expressing her appreciation for my ministry and saying how much over the years she had been helped by the teaching seminars that I had led. This woman had no particular reason to write at that time, and she did not have my address, so she had clearly gone to some trouble to find it. That made her words all the more encouraging and real to me, for behind what she had written I could detect the voice of God, anticipating my need, reminding me of his presence.

Several of the individual words and phrases that David chooses here in Psalm 23 add to our encouragement. "Even though" reminds us that the valley experience is not what we should normally expect, but nevertheless, unusual as it is, it is not outside of God's control. Even in the extremes of Christian experience, God remains constant and faithful, and can be trusted.

"Even though I walk" teaches us that we do not have to run in blind panic when we meet adversity, but can trustingly walk by faith in every circumstance that confronts us. Walking is a common metaphor for the Christian life, and it suggests the measured pace of confidence in God rather than the frantic tizzy of unbelief.

"Even though I walk through" suggests that we will not be in the valley for ever. The experience will have an end, just as it had a beginning. As Julian of Norwich said, "All things will pass," and the Shepherd who leads us into the valley will definitely lead us through it. We may wish to avoid it or skirt round it, but he will lead us through it. Darkness will give way to light; despair will yield to hope. We shall sing again.

"Even though I walk through the valley of the shadow" indicates that many of our fears are not grounded in reality. They are more imagination than truth. Most of our fears never materialize, they are merely shadows and have no real substance to them. Even death is but a shadow when seen in the light of Christ's triumphant resurrection. As Spurgeon said, the shadow of a dog cannot bite you, so why be afraid?

I have called this chapter "The Divine Companion" because that is how David presents the Shepherd to us. A companion is one who accompanies us, who shares the journey with us. Remember how God spoke to Moses? "My Presence will go with you, and I will give you rest" (Exodus 33:14). It is a significant thought to grasp and bring into our thinking. God is with us. In grace he has chosen to share our journey. In grace he stoops down to be alongside us. We need not be afraid if he is our guardian and guide.

14 The Divine Protector

It is very easy, when we are thinking of God as our Shepherd, to become soft and sentimental in our thinking. Emphasizing the love and tender care of God, his gentleness and compassion, can in fact lead us to a lopsided and inadequate understanding of what he is really like. It is a danger that devotional writer J. D. Jones warns about in his meditations on Psalm 23, reminding us that "when we think of God as the Shepherd, we must not emasculate the figure. There is force and vigour and power and authority in it as well as tender love."[11]

Certainly David would not have had any such emasculated notion of God in his mind as he wrote. He knew that a shepherd needed to be strong and brave, as well as tender and compassionate, for he was called upon not just to tend his flock but also to protect them from wild beasts and robbers. Shepherding is not for the faint-hearted, for there are moments of danger when the shepherd needs to be strong and courageous. David had learned this himself on the hillsides outside Bethlehem. He told King Saul, when faced with the challenge of Goliath, "Your servant has been keeping his father's sheep. When a lion or a bear came and carried off a sheep from the flock, I went after it, struck it and rescued the sheep from its mouth. When it turned on me, I seized it by its hair, struck it and killed it. Your servant has killed both the lion and the bear; this uncircumcised Philistine will be like one of them" (1 Samuel 17:34–36).

If we are to enjoy protection, our Shepherd must not only be gentle, but be brave; he must not only be tender, but be strong. It is difficult for us to think of the combination of power and gentleness, strength and tenderness, authority and grace, love and holiness, but in Jesus they are all there in perfect balance. We tend to emphasize one and neglect the other, but he is always both.

David was tender toward his sheep but fearsome toward their enemies. Love alone is insufficient to guarantee our safety. We need a Shepherd who has authority and power as well, who can see off our enemies and guide us safely through the dangerous ravines through which we must pass. In the risen, ascended Jesus we have such a powerful Shepherd.

The importance of keeping a balanced understanding of who God is was brought home to me recently during a Quiet Day I was leading in Singapore. It is an emphasis of my ministry to help people to discover and experience the love of God for themselves, but as I prepared for this particular day, I sensed God saying to me, "Tony, your God is too small." I wasn't quite sure what this meant fully, but it was at the back of my mind as I began the day.

Just after lunch, and as we began the afternoon session, a tropical storm began. Now you need to have experienced a tropical storm to know how suddenly one can come, and how fierce it can be. Thunder boomed above us, and lightning flashed all around. The rain poured down in sheets, deafening in its ferocity. Suddenly a thought came into my mind, a reminder of some advice I had been given for leading retreats or Quiet Days—to make use of whatever happens during the day. So I stopped my talk and asked the participants instead to listen to the storm and see what it said to them.

Some said they felt washed and cleansed as they listened to the rain pouring down. Others said they felt safe and secure, hidden inside the building as the storm raged, reminding them that they were safe in Jesus. As we continued to listen, I suggested that we kneel down and worship the God whose power was being demonstrated to us. It was at that moment that a great sense of the awesomeness of God overwhelmed me. I lay prostrate on the ground, face down, and could not move. It was as if a great weight was resting on me. I lay there for some fifteen minutes, awestruck by the majesty of God, unable to do anything but soak up the presence of the mighty Creator. My wife thought I had gone to sleep! It wasn't that, however. I simply could not get up.

That experience did more to teach me about the fear of the Lord than any number of seminars I could have attended or books I might have read. In that moment, something was burned into my soul—a new appreciation for the greatness of God. I realized I had been in danger of sentimentalizing God, of separating his love from his power. Through the experience of the storm, God was restoring balance to my perception of him. I became aware of the good Shepherd in a new light, full of authority and power and majesty and might, an awesome figure frightening to his enemies but comforting to his sheep.

Any shepherd setting out into the hills to care for his flock would take with him a minimum of equipment. Perhaps he carried a water bottle, maybe a purse, possibly a sling like David's. Certainly he would have with him his rod and his staff. The rod was like a club and was used mainly for defending himself and the flock. The staff—a long, slender stick with a crook or hook on one end—was used to tend the sheep themselves. In the way that David expresses it here, both the rod and the staff bring comfort and reassurance to the sheep.

The rod speaks to us of the authority of Jesus over his enemies. It reminds us that our Shepherd is also a mighty warrior, and that through his death and resurrection he has conquered not only sin and death but also the powers of darkness. As we walk through the valley of deep darkness, there is a sense of the presence of evil. It is a dangerous and frightening place, but we need not be afraid because he is with us. We are comforted by the knowledge that he has overcome, and that he is able to deliver us.

J. O. Fraser was a pioneer missionary among the Lisu, a superstitious people locked in spiritual darkness. The early years of his ministry among them bore little fruit, and he became greatly discouraged. An oppressive darkness swept over his soul as the enormity of the spiritual conflict became apparent to him. One day a magazine arrived for him from England, sent by a friend. As he read, an article in its pages reminded him of the complete victory of Jesus at the cross, and God spoke powerfully to him through these words, drawing his attention to the authority of Jesus. Encouraged by this new revelation, he began to resist the powers of darkness on the basis of Christ's victory, and he found that it worked. The oppression lifted, his mood improved, and, more important, the Lisu gradually became more responsive to the gospel.

Such times of spiritual darkness and oppression are not uncommon, especially for those who seek to bring the gospel to new places or who challenge the hold that darkness has on the lives of others. What we need to remember is that we can apply the victory of Jesus to our lives. We can ask the Shepherd to use his rod and put every demonic power to flight. With him by our side we can dwell in safety and need have no fear.

The staff, more than any other item of equipment, is the thing we most associate with a shepherd, for it is something uniquely used in caring for sheep. It reminds us of the authority of Jesus in our own lives. While it is a symbol of concern, it also represents the discipline and watchfulness that the good Shepherd brings to our lives. Sheep, as we have seen, can be notoriously stubborn and self-willed. There are times when they need a strong hand, and the shepherd must handle them with firmness. We are no different. We need to remember that Christ sometimes takes a strong grip on our lives. As Paul told the wayward Corinthians, "He is not weak in dealing with you, but is powerful among you" (2 Corinthians 13:3).

The staff was used mainly to reach out and catch hold of individual sheep, particularly for close examination to see if there was any disease or wound that might need attention. This watchful care is very reassuring to the sheep and, of course, is the guarantee that they stay healthy. Likewise, the good Shepherd closely watches over our lives, and gives us attention when we need it. He speaks to us through his word, pointing out our need, showing us if we are in danger of losing our way. His word is living and active, sharper than a two-edged sword, convicting us of things that are amiss in our lives, showing us how to put things right. Sometimes it feels as if our very hearts have been laid open before him, that nothing can be hidden from him. We need such correction, however, and it often saves us from trouble later on (see Hebrews 4:12–13; 2 Timothy 3:16–17; 4:2).

The staff was used also to guide the sheep, pointing them gently into the right path, especially where the track was dangerous or difficult. A friendly tap on the sheep's back was a reminder that the shepherd was there and that they were still in touch. It reminds me of how God has sometimes spoken to me through the faithful words of a friend who has brought a timely challenge to me, perhaps urging me to do better in some area of my life, or warning me of some danger ahead. How we need such rebukes, and what a sign they are of real love, the tough love with which God deals with us! As Proverbs tells us, we should not resent such robust treatment, for it is part of God's disciplining of us, and that is a sign of his true, fatherly love (see Proverbs 3:11–12).

The staff also came in handy when a sheep had completely lost its way. Perhaps greedy for one more mouthful of grass, some poor sheep might slip over the edge of a cliff and fall down below. Maybe, in trying to get some extra luscious forage, it might push too far into a wild thornbush and find itself tangled up. Many are the difficulties that sheep create for themselves, and for which there is only one answer—the shepherd's crook. With tenderness and compassion, but with strength of purpose and the wisdom of what is needed to rescue the sheep, the shepherd hooks his staff around the neck or leg and jerks it free. Painful perhaps, but necessary.

The writer to the Hebrews tells us that it is a fearful thing to fall into the hands of the living God (10:31) and that God disciplines us so that we may share in his holiness (12:7–11). He loves us too much to see us make a mess of our lives, and is not afraid to intervene strongly if necessary to save us from ourselves. He will even use hardship to draw us back to him, shaping the circumstances of life so that they remind us of our need of him. Like the prodigal son, he will allow us to come to the end of ourselves if it will bring us back to our senses. He is not afraid to cause us pain if it will save us from ruin. This is tough love indeed, but paradoxically it is the guarantee of our acceptance, the sign that we are truly his children.

The word *comfort* is a word that has lost some of its meaning in modern usage. Nowadays it has a soft sense, speaking of solace, of ease, of gentle soothing. Originally it was a much sharper word, being made up of two Latin words, *cum* and *forte,* which literally meant *with strength.* To comfort someone meant to put strength into them, to give them the backbone to carry on, to fortify them, and to strengthen their resolve. This is the kind of comfort David has in mind when he speaks of the rod and staff.

Personally speaking, I know I need that kind of comfort. I am grateful for a God who loves me enough to save me from my own foolishness. I find it reassuring to know that God is there, watching over my life, and that he will not easily let me go. It makes me feel secure to know that he will intervene, both to deliver me from my enemies and to rescue me from my own mistakes. Like David, I find comfort in the presence of the Shepherd, with his rod and his staff to guide and to guard me. Not only do I have a divine companion to journey with me, I have a divine protector watching over me.

15 Fear No Evil

Any experience of the valley is likely to raise questions in our minds. We can find ourselves in such pain and heartache that we are bound to cry, "Does God love me? Does he really care?" These are the honest questions of our heart, and we would be wrong to dismiss them lightly. Unheard and unanswered, they can leave us angry and dissatisfied.

In describing the valley, David hints at the presence of evil, although he does not fear it. He himself had often suffered at the hands of evil men, and must have been aware, as we all are, of the presence in the world of a malevolent evil force, which the Bible calls the devil. One of the greatest questions that has faced the church throughout its history is this: if there is a God of love, why is there so much suffering in the world? It raises other issues too. If God is all-powerful, why doesn't he step into the world to prevent wars and famines and earthquakes? Why do bad things happen to good people, yet those who are wicked seem to get away with it? Why does so much suffering seem unjust and pointless?

These are real dilemmas that have taxed the minds of the greatest thinkers and theologians. They become very immediate when we are personally involved in tragedy, and pain and suffering come knocking on our own door. It would be extremely presumptuous of me to think that I had the answers to these questions. I do not pretend to be so wise! I am often as baffled as anyone else. In thirty years of pastoral ministry, though, I have been forced to face these questions again and again, sometimes as questioner, sometimes as the one being questioned. I do not have any final answers, only a few pointers that have helped me, in some small way, to arrive at least at a working approach to the problem, and to be able to continue to trust God despite the many pieces of the jigsaw of life that do not seem to fit. Like everyone else, I wait for heaven and the final explanation, and the completion of the puzzle.

One important thing to say at the beginning is that there is only a problem if there is a God of love. If there is no God, then of course we are left at the mercy of random forces and can have no expectation that things should turn out well for us. Further, if there is a God and he is less than good (capricious, unfeeling, detached), then we should not be surprised if he allows bad things to happen to us, or maybe even laughs at our suffering, for why should he care? Only a God who is love would care. So, in a strange way, the very existence of the question in our minds suggests that in our hearts we know there is a God, and that if he is there, he must be good. Otherwise, there is no problem.

The problem does remain, however, and presents us with what Brennan Manning calls an "enormous difficulty." He writes:

> The ubiquitous presence of pain and suffering—unwanted, apparently undeserved, and not amenable to explanation and remedy—poses an enormous obstacle to unfailing trust in the infinite goodness of God. How does one dare to propose the way of trust in the face of raw, undifferentiated heartache, cosmic disorder, and the terror of history?[12]

In other words, how can those of us who believe in a God of love make sense of it all? Can we really trust the Shepherd?

Here are some of the waymarks that have guided me on my journey so far.

Firstly, we must recognize that we live in a fallen world and among fallen people, and even as believers we are not immune to the pain and hurt that this world throws at us. Faith is not a divine guarantee that nothing unpleasant will ever happen to us. Believing is not a heavenly insurance policy against disaster. I know that many people wish it were so, and that sometimes unscrupulous religious teachers sell the gospel in this way, but authentic Christianity recognizes that suffering is inevitable.

Thus, during the early days of the SARS outbreak in the Far East, a good and faithful church leader was asked to pray for a young woman mysteriously ill in hospital. He himself caught the virus and died soon afterward, while the young woman recovered. It seems unfair that a person whose only motivation was to serve others should die like that, but it is an example of what is involved in living in a fallen world. When bad things happen to good people, it doesn't mean they have sinned, or that they are being punished by God. It is simply that they too are caught up in tragic events of life.

Secondly, we believe that God is able to take situations and events that seem evil and somehow work them into his overall good purpose for us. This is the clear biblical perspective given to us by Paul. His own life and ministry were full of suffering and hardship, yet he never lost sight of this perspective: "And we know that in all things God works for the good of those who love him, who have been called according to his purpose" (Romans 8:28). This clear and unmistakable truth has been the rock on which countless believers down the centuries have rested their faith in times of trial. It has been the compass by which they have navigated their way through the stormy seas of life. It has been their watchword in time of need, their light in the darkness. Whatever has come our way—trouble or hardship, persecution or famine, nakedness, danger or sword—we can overcome these difficulties in the knowledge that nothing can separate us from the love of God that is in Christ Jesus our Lord. This is Paul's bold assertion, and it has been the proven testimony of thousands of others ever since (see Romans 8:28–39).

The reason we are able to keep on trusting God despite what happens to us is that this truth provides a framework for our understanding. Events are not as random as they may seem: there is ultimately a pattern behind them. Corrie Ten Boom once visited a man in the hospital who was in an iron lung. In order to help him make some sense of his pain, she showed him her embroidery. One side was a meaningless jumble of threads and knots. Turning it over, however, she revealed a picture of a beautiful crown. Her meaning was clear. Sometimes we can only see the threads and knots, but God has a clearer picture. He is weaving even the most difficult events of our lives into his overall design for us, something which, when completed, will be beautiful and pleasing to him.

A third biblical insight into the question of suffering is the realization that adversity can actually produce something good within us—that is, if we respond to it positively. It does something for our character. Again, we look to Paul for insight. "We rejoice in our sufferings," he says, "because we know that suffering produces perseverance; perseverance, character; and character, hope" (Romans 5:3–4). Some years ago, author Paul Bilheimer wrote a little book called *Don't Waste Your Sorrows*. The title itself challenges us not to lose ourselves in self-pity, but to allow God to produce something of lasting benefit out of our difficult days. As counselor Selwyn Hughes often says, we have the choice to become bitter or to become better.

Margaret was a Chinese friend of ours when we were missionaries in Sarawak. A victim of polio, she has been crippled from her youth, and her superstitious parents (thinking they had offended the gods) gave her away to be brought up in a Salvation Army home. As she grew up, confined to a wheelchair, she learned to sew and do dressmaking. Although later she was allowed back into the family home, she was despised and picked on continually. Life was very difficult for her, but she never grumbled or complained. Instead she allowed her sufferings to make her more compassionate, and appreciated every kindness that was shown to her. She was one of those people who, when you visit to cheer them up, end up making you feel better! Despite her poverty she was generous, often pushing a crumpled dollar note into my hand as a gift. Margaret didn't waste her sorrows; she built on them and let them produce something beautiful in her life that may not have been there without her adversity.

One final perspective from scripture adds to our understanding. What suffering does is to loosen us from the grip of this world and create in us a longing for the next. Paul, who suffered as much as most, looked at it like this. "For our light and momentary troubles are achieving for us an eternal glory that far outweighs them all. So we fix our eyes not on what is seen, but on what is unseen" (2 Corinthians 4:17–18). He compared life on earth to living in a tent, a frail and fragile existence, which makes us groan and long for our more permanent and abiding home in heaven. If we are comfortable and at ease in this life, we may easily lose our grip on the fact that this life is not our real home. A certain amount of dis-ease in the world rightly keeps our focus on what is yet to be. It helps us to keep eternity in view.

Many of the great African American spirituals were written by those who were slaves, who longed for the freedom of heaven. Their suffering and oppression caused them to reach out to God in song, yearning for the better place of which the Bible speaks, that place where there is no more mourning or death or crying or pain. They trusted even in the harshest of circumstances.

Can we trust the Shepherd? I believe we can, even when we cannot understand everything. It would be nice to have explanations and ready-made solutions for every problem. Many of us would like to be able to put God in a box and systematize and predict his every action. God, however, is God and will not be confined by human understanding. He is too great for that. His wisdom is beyond comprehension, his paths beyond tracing out. He does not need us to counsel him or to tell him how he should act. We shall have to learn to live with mystery, to be humble enough to leave some of our questions unanswered, and to love him just the same.

At the end of the day, what is required is a simple act of trusting obedience. I have to believe that the good Shepherd really is good, even if I do not understand all his ways, and even if sometimes life is unbearably painful. I have to take him at his word. "Trust in God; trust also in me" (John 14:1).

We can then pray in the way Brennan Manning suggests.

> When they [our many and varied fears] threaten to consume us, we can overpower them with a simple and deliberate act of trust: "Jesus, by your grace I grow still for a moment and I hear you say, 'Courage! It's me! Don't be afraid.' I place my trust in your presence and your love. Thank you."[13]

Questions for Reflection

For individuals

1. In what ways has God guided you in the past? Think back over events in your life. What have been the key moments, and what have you learned through them?

2. Have there been any "valley" experiences in your life? How did you cope?

3. How do you understand "trust" in this context? Why does it need to be "ruthless"? For what might you need to trust God at this moment?

4. In what ways have you experienced the divine companionship?

5. Is there any sense in which your God may be too small?

6. Do you have any doubts in your heart about the goodness of God? How can you resolve them? Does chapter 15 help in any way?

For groups

1. What do you think is meant by "the radical nature of discipleship"?

2. What are some of the common ways in which God guides us? How does God speak to us? What are the safety checks in guidance?

3. How are we to understand the "valley" experience? What might it involve? Why does it happen? How does God help?

4. Discuss Brennan Manning's statement: "It may mean more to Jesus when we say 'I trust you' than when we say 'I love you.'"

5. How do we know that God is with us? How has his presence been "fleshed out" for you?

6. What is the purpose of God's discipline?

7. What questions do you have about suffering and evil? Do any of the biblical perspectives shared in chapter 15 help?

4

Learning to Live

You prepare a table before me in the presence of
my enemies. You anoint my head with oil; my
cup overflows. Surely goodness and love will
follow me all the days of my life, and I will dwell
in the house of the Lord for ever. (vv. 5–6)

໑

*To live the Christian life effectively, we need to learn
how to live from the resources of God rather than from
our own strength. God in Christ has provided
everything we need to do his will. The important thing
now is to exchange our ability for his.*

16 A Table Prepared

Although not all commentators agree, it seems that there is a change in the metaphor being used at this point in the psalm (v. 5). The shepherd imagery is replaced by that of the gracious host who, as our friend, now welcomes us to his banqueting table. The scene also moves from the outdoors of the countryside to the interior and splendid surroundings of the palace. We notice a mood shift as well. The danger and apprehension of the valley has given way to the joy and celebration of a festive occasion.

Those writers who are familiar with shepherding inevitably try to press the imagery all the way through, but it seems forced and unnatural. The more detached Bible scholars almost unanimously agree that we are now thinking in terms of the king who, in his generosity, invites us to sit at his table. If we remember that David was both a shepherd and a king, there seems no problem in accepting a change of metaphor. Jesus, of course, fits both descriptions perfectly, a fact brought out in Henry W. Baker's well-known hymn "The King of Love My Shepherd Is."

To sit at the king's table is a privilege indeed, and David was a man given to generous hospitality. The story of how he invited the helpless Mephibosheth to have a regular place at his table illustrates his magnanimity (2 Samuel 9). As the grandson of his enemy Saul, some would have expected David to have Mephibosheth put to death. As one crippled in both legs and unable to support himself financially, others would have seen him as a burden and drain on resources. Mephibosheth himself is surprised at David's invitation, saying, "What is your servant that you should notice a dead dog like me?" But out of love for his father, Jonathan (David's loyal friend), and in order to show God's kindness, David insists that room be made at the royal table for the unlikeliest of guests.

Doesn't this show what grace is all about? God has invited us to share in the riches of his provision even though we are weak and utterly undeserving. In his mercy he has given us a place at his table when he is under no obligation whatever to do so. We are surprised by his kindness, taken aback by his generosity. The more we understand grace, the more we realize how truly amazing it is.

The table spread before us represents all the benefits of the finished work of Christ. In some ways we are seeing here a repeat of the thought of verse 1—that God has provided everything that we need. It is a thought well worth repeating, for we have to learn how to live in the benefit of it. A very real danger for us is that, having started the Christian life in grace, we then try to live it in our own strength. A subtle transfer takes place, moving us out of grace and into "works," by which we mean activities done in our own energy.

According to Paul, the Christian path requires an "exchanged" life, which can only be lived when we draw on the resources available to us in Christ. In fact, it is true to say that there is only one person who can actually live the Christian life, and that is Christ himself. The one who gave his life for us now offers to live his life in us, and then through us. The apostle's great statement on how to live the Christian life is worthy of prayerful meditation. "I have been crucified with Christ," he says, "and I no longer live, but Christ lives in me. The life I live in the body, I live by faith in the Son of God, who loved me and gave himself for me" (Galatians 2:19–20). Only God's Spirit can reveal to us exactly what this means, and how it is to be worked out in our individual lives, but it provides a crucial insight about how we can, in practice, live the life that God has called us to. God does not merely want to change my life; his desire is to exchange it for his own.

What is it that God has spread before us? Of what does the banquet consist? Set before us are all the benefits that flow from Christ's atoning death on the cross and victorious resurrection—in other words, everything that is associated with our salvation and is needed in order to live the Christian life on a daily basis. Several New Testament scriptures express the completeness of God's provision and its present availability to those who believe.

Perhaps the best starting point is Ephesians 1:3: "Praise be to the God and Father of our Lord Jesus Christ, who has blessed us in the heavenly realms with every spiritual blessing in Christ." Here we see that we have already been given every spiritual blessing. Included are those things that establish our relationship with God (reconciliation, redemption, forgiveness, cleansing, pardon, eternal life, and so on), as well as what we need to live out the new life (strength, power, wisdom, discernment, perseverance, and so on), and what makes the new life so worthwhile (love, joy, peace, and so on). These things are already ours. They have been given to us in Christ and are the resources we need.

A similar thought is found in 2 Peter 1:3: "His divine power has given us everything we need for life and godliness through our knowledge of him who called us by his own glory and goodness." Again we notice the fact that we already have what we need to live in a godly way. The resources are available; we do not have to try to find them ourselves or work them up from within ourselves. They are ours in Christ.

Another verse in Colossians adds to the picture of an abundant provision already made available to us: "For in Christ all the fullness of the Deity dwells in bodily form, and you have been given fullness in Christ" (Colossians 2:9–10). The King James Version puts it more directly—"You are complete in him"—a wonderful statement of encouragement and hope. Through our relationship with Christ we do not lack in any way.

Imagine I deposited a thousand dollars into your bank account and the next day you received a bill for fifty dollars. Would you be worried? I don't think so. You would know you already had what was needed to meet that expense. You would go to the bank, draw upon your resources and pay the bill. This is exactly what God has done for us. He has paid into our account all that we need to do his will. Whenever we have a need for strength or grace or whatever, we simply turn to him in prayer and draw on our spiritual resources. As we do that, his very life (the life of Christ) flows into us afresh, imparting to us exactly what we need at that moment.

Dependency on God becomes, then, an essential part of living the life that he has for us. It is something God is constantly teaching us, creating in us the awareness that we cannot do it without him (John 15:5). Our weakness becomes God's opportunity, for it is our failure and inadequacy that allows him room to work within us, to perfect his strength in our weakness (2 Corinthians 12:7–10). It may be that one of the reasons why God leads us through difficult and dark valleys is to expose the insufficiency of our own resources, making us rely not on ourselves but on him. Perhaps he has to break the stubborn self-reliance in each of us in order that his life may be seen more fully in us (see 2 Corinthians 1:9).

No matter how many times we come to God and draw on his resources, there is always a sufficient supply. We need not fear to come again and again, because he delights in supplying everything we need. "From the fullness of his grace we have all received one blessing after another" (John 1:16). *The Message* emphasizes the sheer generosity of God implied in this verse: "We all live off his generous bounty, gift after gift after gift." He never tires of giving, and delights to exchange his life for ours.

The story is told of a poor man who longed to have a holiday aboard a cruise ship. He scrimped and saved for many years and eventually had enough to buy a ticket for a month-long voyage. Unfortunately he had little money left, and he feared he would not be able to pay for his food on board, so he took with him a simple supply of cheese and biscuits. Each day when the other passengers went to dine at the ship's table, he would disappear to a quiet corner and munch his cheese and crackers. He was envious of the others, but at least he was on board.

One day, one of the ship's officers noticed him. "Sir," he said, "why don't you come and eat at the ship's table with the other passengers? The food is really excellent."

Embarrassed, the man replied, "I'm afraid I can't afford the prices at your fancy restaurant. You see, I'm just a poor man. But don't worry about me, I'm happy with my cheese and biscuits."

The officer looked astonished. "But sir," he said, "don't you realize that all your meals are included in the price of your ticket? You don't have to pay anything more. Everything has already been provided. Come, let me show you to your table."

How easy it is for us to fail to realize that God has already provided all that we need in Christ, and to deprive ourselves of the blessing that is ours through him. The king of love invites us to his table. No false modesty should hold us back, no sense of unworthiness keep us from taking our place. Not even our adversaries can prevent us enjoying what he has provided for us, for this table is spread "in the presence of my enemies."

David had many enemies during the course of his life, and, even at the time of writing this psalm, he may have been fleeing for his life from his son Absalom. He knew what it was to be hunted down, to be pursued like an animal in the desert, to be the focus of hatred and hostility. Yet God had never allowed his enemies to take his life. Often he had found God's provision and supply in the most unexpected places, to the annoyance of those who sought his life.

Although we may not find ourselves in such a position, we do, of course, have spiritual enemies. Satan and the powers of darkness are arrayed against us, and seek our destruction, but they are held back by the power of God. They cannot harm us, for Christ has triumphed over them at the cross, disarming them and rendering them ineffective (see Colossians 2:15). We can take our place at God's banqueting table without any fear. All they can do is to look on in frustration and defeat.

In John Bunyan's *Pilgrim's Progress*, Pilgrim comes at one point on his journey to a place where two ferocious lions guard the way. At first he can see no way to pass them safely, but then notices that they are chained, and that if he keeps to the path, they cannot reach him. They may growl and roar, and he may feel frightened and afraid, but they cannot actually harm him. There is something of that thought in the fact that we take our seat in the presence of our enemies. No matter what accusations, lies, or intimidating threats Satan may throw at us, he cannot prevent us from receiving God's supply of blessing. As Paul rightly observed, "If God is for us, who can be against us?" (Romans 8:31).

Do you require strength? You have it. Do you lack wisdom? It is yours already. Do you need forgiveness? It is there in abundance. Are you longing for more joy? It is set before you. Are you lacking in peace? Accept it freely, for it has been provided in ample measure. Everything we need and more is already ours. We simply stretch out our hands and receive by faith, with thanksgiving, whatever we need from the table of divine provision. The gracious host has anticipated our need and made adequate arrangements. We are free to enjoy his wonderful hospitality.

17 Living in the Anointing

As the metaphor of the gracious host unfolds before us, we see next that our divine friend receives us into his presence in such a way that we feel welcomed and accepted. He anoints our head with oil to show that we are special to him, and then fills our cup to overflowing, reminding us of his generosity. We may inwardly feel unworthy to sit at the king's table, and be nervous in his presence, but for his part he is at pains to ensure that we feel at home there, and can relax.

Anointing was a familiar custom in Israel. Kings were anointed, and so were priests, marking them as set apart for God. David could look back fondly to the day of his own anointing. Samuel the prophet had arrived at the family home unannounced, and with some special purpose in mind that only he seemed to know. Unbeknown to the family, he had come to anoint the next king, in succession to Saul.

Having inspected the older brothers first, and for some reason not being satisfied with any of them, he had called for David (the youngest) to be brought before him. David came in from tending the sheep to be greeted by the prophet, who immediately recognized that he was the one whom God had chosen. There and then, in the presence of his family, he anointed him with oil, identifying him as the next king of Israel (see 1 Samuel 16:1–13).

From that moment, the Holy Spirit came upon David in power. He was never the same again. God had marked him out for his own purpose, and had given him a divine ability to fulfill the task he had been given. Throughout his life David depended on the anointing, on the presence and empowering, of the Spirit. The reason he could shepherd the people of Israel so skillfully was that he continually relied on the help of the Spirit. For the same reason, God has given the Holy Spirit to us. We can do the things God wants us to do only because the Holy Spirit is with us. We depend not on our own strength but on his power.

Anointing was also a sign of welcome. Honored guests were anointed with perfume out of respect and love. This Eastern custom may also have been in David's mind as he wrote. We can also see its importance in one of the Gospel stories. Jesus had been invited to the house of a Pharisee to eat. During the meal, a woman known for her immoral lifestyle dramatically interrupted the proceedings. She broke open an alabaster jar and poured perfume on Jesus, wetting his feet with her tears and wiping them with her hair. It was an unrestrained demonstration of love and affection, the response of one who had been forgiven much.

Simon, the host, was outraged by such a performance from one so despised, but Jesus took a different view. He reminded Simon that, compared to the woman, he had been negligent in his welcome. "I came into your house. You did not give me any water for my feet, but she wet my feet with her tears and wiped them with her hair. You did not give me a kiss, but this woman, from the time I entered, has not stopped kissing my feet. You did not put oil on my head, but she has poured perfume on my feet" (Luke 7:44–46).

We can be sure that there is nothing lacking in the welcome given to us by God. His hospitality is faultless. Our gracious host anoints our head with oil—that is, he bestows the Holy Spirit on us as the guarantee of our acceptance and welcome. Not only does the Holy Spirit enable us to do the will of God, he also assures us that we are loved by God and are his special guests (see Romans 8:15–16).

In the anointing of which David speaks, both these truths are implied. God gives his Spirit to us, empowering us to live for him and assuring us of his love. This anointing is something that takes place at our conversion. It happens at the moment of the new birth, and therefore, if we are believers, it is something that has already happened to us. It is not something we need to search for, an elusive blessing constantly held out in front of us, available only to a select few. Rather, it is something we already have but must grow into.

Paul made this clear to the church at Corinth. First of all, he emphasizes the divine initiative that is always the identifying mark of grace: "Now it is God who makes both us and you stand firm in Christ." Then he reminds the believers of the provision God has already made for them: "He anointed us, set his seal of ownership on us, and put his Spirit in our hearts as a deposit, guaranteeing what is to come" (2 Corinthians 1:21–22). Notice that Paul uses the past tense: "He anointed us. . . ." Paul is speaking of something that has already happened, an accomplished fact that we are to accept by faith.

By giving us his Spirit, God has set his seal of ownership upon us. He has marked us out as belonging to himself. That is something that he recognizes, that evil will recognize, and that we know too. It is what Romans 8:15–16 calls "the witness of the Spirit," and it creates the "blessed assurance" of which Fanny J. Crosby wrote. It is what determines our new identity in Christ, for we are those who belong to God and have been marked out as his special people. Furthermore, by placing the Spirit in our hearts, he has guaranteed that this is only the start of the blessing he intends to give to us.

The presence of the Spirit is the down-payment, the first installment. Wonderful as this life is, the best is yet to be.

Another way of looking at this is to remember that Jesus is the Christ, which literally means "the Anointed One." He was the Messiah promised from of old, who would come to save God's people and who would do so in the power of the Spirit. When he stood up in the synagogue at Nazareth and read from the prophet Isaiah, he was fulfilling this expectation. "The Spirit of the Lord is on me," he said, "because he has anointed me to preach good news to the poor" (Luke 4:18). Then, having finished his work on earth and ascended to the right hand of God, he was demonstrated to be both Lord and Christ. The outpouring of the Spirit on the day of Pentecost was the visible proof of his position. Peter explained it this way: "Exalted to the right hand of God, he has received from the Father the promised Holy Spirit and has poured out what you now see and hear" (Acts 2:33).

If Jesus is the Anointed One, and we are in him, then it follows that we share in his anointing. I am anointed because he is anointed. The Holy Spirit flows from him to me. When this happens, he is in fact sharing his very life with us. Pentecost marked the initial outpouring of the Spirit, and believers ever since have lived in the benefit of that momentous event.

Having been anointed by the Spirit, we must then learn to live in the reality of it, to grow into it. We have the Holy Spirit, but the most important question is, "Does the Holy Spirit have us?" That is, do we make ourselves available to him; are we responsive to his promptings; will we obey his leading? It is this yielding of ourselves to the Spirit that leads to our being filled with the Spirit (Ephesians 5:18), which is the basis of the normal Christian life. As we offer ourselves to God unreservedly, the Holy Spirit's gracious influence is released more and more fully in our lives. He gives us power to do God's will, imparts to us the gifts we need to serve him, and produces within us the lovely fruit of the Spirit. Day by day, as we give ourselves afresh to God, the anointing continues to flow, making us fruitful and effective in our service for him. With a growing awareness of his presence and sensitivity to his voice, we learn to live in the anointing.

Dr. R. T. Kendall, who was for many years the minister at Westminster Chapel, a well-known church in London, has written and spoken much about the importance of God's anointing upon our lives. This respected Bible teacher is clear about the need to live within the anointing. "Next to the gift of salvation and the sure knowledge that we will go to heaven when we die," he writes, "the anointing is our most precious possession."[14] David, too, was aware of its importance, and feared that after his sin with Bathsheba the Spirit might be taken from him. Earnestly he cried to God, "Do not cast me from your presence or take your Holy Spirit from me" (Psalm 51:11). He could not imagine trying to live without the Spirit's enabling.

Are there obstructions to the anointing? Clearly there are. Unconfessed sin will limit the flow of God's power to our lives. Bitterness, resentment, and anger in particular seem to short-circuit the movement of the Spirit. Unbelief creates a blockage too. Some people feel unworthy to receive such a gift, thinking that they are not good enough for something they associate with the spiritual elite. They forget that it is a gift of grace and totally undeserved by anyone. Some perhaps quench the working of the Spirit because of their personal fear, shyness, or inhibition; others refuse to submit themselves to God, and their wills remain unbroken, limiting their availability to God. Often we lack anointing on our lives simply because we are too busy to spend time waiting on God.

Carol was a young woman who loved God sincerely and wanted to grow in her Christian life. She was aware of her need of the Holy Spirit's help in her life, but whenever people prayed for her to receive the Holy Spirit, nothing much seemed to happen. Some blamed her for her lack of faith, others urged her to keep seeking until she received the elusive blessing.

One evening she was alone in her room, thinking about all this, when it suddenly dawned on her that she already had the Holy Spirit. Why, then, did she need to keep searching for something she already had? Quietly, she began to thank God for giving the Holy Spirit to her. As she did this, the love of God began to sweep over her in waves, gently at first, then much more strongly, causing this normally shy and reserved young woman to burst out into joyful laughter. She knew then that she had been filled with the Spirit, and the experience became a watershed in her Christian growth.

Once we have the revelation in our hearts that we have already been anointed with the Spirit, it only requires a step of faith to begin to allow the Spirit to work within us. Once we believe that he is already present, it is not difficult to trust that he will enable and empower us in the situations that we face. This is how we learn to live, depending each day on the Spirit who dwells within us.

18 Living in the Overflow

Without the anointing of the Holy Spirit, the Christian life is hard work. We become drained and weary, and feel empty inside. It feels as if we are running on empty. When this happens, we need to remember the second of David's statements: "my cup overflows." It is not God's will for us to remain dried up and parched. His desire is to pour his life into us in such abundance that we are not just full, but overflowing.

Counselors sometimes speak of what they call "deficit motivation." It describes a situation where, because some people's own deepest needs remain unmet, they look to other people to meet those needs. This means that they can never give into a relationship; they can only take from it. It is as if their own well is dry, and they are looking to others to supply what is missing. Such people, we are told, become manipulative in their relationships, draining life from those around them.

God is the only one who can meet the deep, inner needs that we have for security, worth, and significance. He meets them by sharing with us his own life, giving to us "living water," as Jesus called it. To the Samaritan woman he met at the well, and who was searching for fulfillment in sexual encounters, he said, "Everyone who drinks this water will be thirsty again, but whoever drinks the water I give him will never thirst. Indeed, the water I give him will become in him a spring of water welling up to eternal life" (John 4:13–14).

The "living water" refers, of course, to the life-giving Holy Spirit who satisfies the thirst of our souls by filling us with the life of God. Again, according to Paul, we see that at the moment of our conversion the Spirit was made available to us. "For we were all baptized by one Spirit into one body—whether Jews or Greeks, slave or free—and we were all given the one Spirit to drink" (1 Corinthians 12:13). So, when we read that the gracious host fills our cup to overflowing, we understand that once more it has to do with imparting the vitality of the Spirit into our hearts and lives. And if we prefer to think of our cup being filled with wine, we come to the same conclusion, for wine in scripture always speaks of the effervescent, bubbling life of God that gladdens the heart.

There is no need, then, for us to live with an empty cup, or even one that is half full. Nor is a brimming cup to be our limit. This generous host wants to fill our cup so that it overflows, spilling out and touching those around us. There is no deficit motivation here! God wants to touch my life so abundantly that not only are my own needs met, but I have spare capacity with which to bless the lives of others. I am meant to live out of an overflow, where the life of God wells up within me and flows out from me like a river (John 7:37–39).

Paul was aware that the grace of God had been poured out on him abundantly, taking the blasphemer, persecutor, and violent man that he was and transforming him into an effective servant of God (1 Timothy 1:12–14). It was as if a river had overflowed its banks, and he had been caught in the deluge. As far as Paul was concerned, everyone who believes has been caught in that same torrent of divine mercy. "For if the many died by the trespass of the one man, how much more did God's grace and the gift that came by the grace of the one man, Jesus Christ, overflow to the many!" (Romans 5:15).

Since we have been caught in this gracious overflow, we can now give ourselves in service to others. Finding our own needs increasingly satisfied in Christ, we are more able to give ourselves freely to others. We can love, for example, because we know that we ourselves are loved by God. We no longer need to do things for others in order to be loved and appreciated by them (which is manipulation), but are liberated to care for them without wanting anything in return (which is ministry). So Paul can pray for the Thessalonian believers like this: "May the Lord make your love increase and overflow for each other and for everyone else, just as ours does for you" (1 Thessalonians 3:12). If we try to love others from our own resources, we shall soon find that our cup is empty. When we depend on the Spirit, and the life of God within us, we discover that we can keep on loving even in the most negative of circumstances. It is a supernatural overflow that is required.

Because we can overflow in love, we can overflow in thanksgiving. The experience of knowing that we are loved unconditionally by God brings healing to our innermost beings, and turns us into positive people who can see good in everything around. No longer weighed down by feelings of rejection and shame, we are set free from the negativity that makes people grumble and complain and find fault with others. Now we can recognize God's goodness in so many places around us, and our lives spill over with thanksgiving (see Colossians 2:6–7).

Because we can overflow with thanksgiving, we can also overflow with hope. We dare to believe that in the midst of darkness and despair there is a way through. We find a confident expectation of good welling up within us, and overflowing into our speech and attitudes. Pessimism turns into optimism. We know that God is working all things together for our good, and that ultimately we shall understand his purposes. This is not the super-optimism of the self-made person, but the working of the Spirit within us. It is what Paul prayed for his friends in Rome: "May the God of hope fill you with all joy and peace as you trust in him, so that you may overflow with hope by the power of the Holy Spirit" (Romans 15:13).

The overflow of hope means that we can overflow with joy. During the first century, the churches in Macedonia experienced severe trials, undergoing persecution and experiencing extreme poverty, yet they did not become miserable or discouraged. Rather, according to Paul, the grace of God was so much with them that in the midst of it all, their overflowing joy welled up into an amazing expression of generosity. When they heard of the financial needs of the believers in Jerusalem, they gave freely and without any compulsion to the offering that Paul was organizing. Indeed, they gave beyond their means, sacrificially contributing to the needs of others and considering it a privilege (see 2 Corinthians 8:1–5). That is supernatural living. In a material world, obsessed with consumerism, such joyful generosity can happen only when people are living in the overflow of God's Spirit.

Added to this, the overflow of joy means that we can overflow with comfort. As believers, we are not spared from painful trials. At one time while in Ephesus, Paul and his friends came under such hardship and stress that they felt they were not going to make it. They almost gave up, but God saw them through. Encouraged by this, they were in turn able to encourage others, for this is how God works and prepares us to help others. Even in their pain there was an overflow. "For just as the sufferings of Christ flow over into our lives, so also through Christ our comfort overflows" (2 Corinthians 1:5). In God's economy, nothing is wasted. If we allow him, he can take our own painful experiences (such as loss, bereavement, illness, redundancy, and so on), and use them so that we can pass on the comfort we have received to others. It is part of the amazing, overflowing life that is released when we allow the Holy Spirit to work through us.

When we find that our cup is empty, what should we do? When we feel we have no more to give, to whom should we turn? We look again to our gracious host, aware of his goodness and generosity, and we lift up our empty cup for him to fill once more. And fill it he most certainly will.

Rachel had been through a very hard time in her life. Her husband had been ill for many months, and she had nursed him through the last stages of his illness. At the same time, things had been difficult in her local church, and with all the other pressures upon her she began to drift away and lose touch. Feeling physically and emotionally drained, she found it hard to come to terms with bereavement. Whereas once her faith had been a source of great strength to her, now she felt spiritually dry, shriveled up inside.

Eventually, through the faithfulness of her friends, Rachel found her way back to church again. It was hard at first, because God seemed so far away, but slowly she began to find her heart opening up. She longed for the kind of closeness with God that she had once known. Then one Sunday, during the time of worship, it happened. She literally cried out to God for his help, and went forward for prayer. It was her way of lifting up her empty cup. Nothing spectacular happened during the time of prayer, but afterward things were different. She began to feel God's presence again, and the hunger to read his word returned. She started to pray once more, and was able to worship more freely. Her attitude became much more positive, and her joy and sense of humor returned. She was beginning to live again in the overflow of God.

Nothing draws the heart of God more toward his people than their humble cry for help. He knows we cannot live the kind of life he has planned for us in our own resources. Of course, like Rachel, there will be times when we run dry. Inevitably we shall come to an end of what we can do. That is the place to which he calls us, for there in the place of emptiness he can fill us afresh, pouring his own divine life into the cup that is our weak, human life.

19 Living Confidently

The whole of Psalm 23 breathes a note of confidence and assurance, but nowhere as clearly as in verse 6. David declares, "Surely goodness and love will follow me all the days of my life." Everything he knows about God as shepherd and host comes together in this bold assertion of continuing care and provision.

It is the word *surely* that strikes us. Not possibly or maybe, or even hopefully, but surely—the confident and certain belief that God's love and mercy will be with him throughout his life, no matter what a day may bring, and no matter how he may respond. It is the language of faith, born out of the repeated experience of God's faithfulness. It is the vocabulary of grace, learned in the school of life. Not for David a life lived defensively, nervously anticipating setbacks, timidly avoiding possible failure. Rather a life lived on the offensive, expecting to see God's goodness no matter what challenges life may throw up, confident of divine resources to meet each new demand.

Some writers see a return to the shepherd imagery at this point, and see *goodness* and *love* as the sheepdogs who round up the flock and keep them on track. The shepherd goes before them, but the dogs come after, following the sheep and ensuring that they don't stray. Other commentators, like F. B. Meyer, see them as guardian angels. "We are well escorted," he says, "with a Shepherd in front and twin angels behind. Someone called them watch-dogs, but I prefer to think of them as angels."[15] Both interpretations are a little fanciful, but they make the point that goodness and love are not just abstract qualities but concrete expressions of God's proactive love at work in our lives.

This is further brought out by the word translated *follow*, which could also be given as *pursue* or even *hunt*. David had often found himself pursued by his enemies, but now he realizes that even in those dark and dangerous moments the love of God relentlessly hunts him down. It was this thought that gave Francis Thompson (1859–1907) the inspiration to write his poem "The Hound of Heaven." He speaks of his own flight from God, and of the seeking and redeeming love of God that pursued him down the years, the footsteps of grace that never gave up the chase until he was at last captured by Love.

Love speaks of the attitude of God toward us, while goodness speaks of the tangible expressions of that love in our lives. The word for *love* is often translated as *mercy* or *loving kindness*, and speaks of the faithful covenant love of God, a love that never gives up on us, and that remains constant despite our inconsistency.

Love and goodness are the Old Testament equivalents of mercy and grace in the New Testament, and are the bedrock on which our relationship with God rests.

Mercy and grace belong together. It is often said that in mercy God does not give us what we do deserve, while in grace God gives us what we don't deserve. The danger of emphasizing the grace of God is that we forget that, first of all, we need mercy. Grace without an understanding of the need for mercy becomes cheap and easily taken for granted. Mercy reminds us that we are sinners deserving of punishment. Our only cry can be, "God, be merciful to me a sinner." The fact that God responds to our cry for help in mercy is to do with the beauty of his character, not any merit in ourselves. "No one has a right to mercy. When we understand this fact and its implications, we gain a deeper appreciation of God's goodness to us."[16]

David had received God's mercy throughout his life, but never more so than after his affair with Bathsheba and his scandalous treatment of her husband, Uriah. Adultery and murder were both on his record, and yet God in his mercy forgave him and wiped out his sin. Bruised and broken, he was free to begin again, although the consequences of his sin continued to trouble him. Yet in Psalm 23 David is not looking backwards. His eye is on the future. Goodness and mercy will follow him into a future as yet unknown, where there will be other temptations, other trials. His confidence is not in himself, but in a caring God who will continue to sustain him despite his weakness and unworthiness. "And today," he once said with insight, "though I am the anointed king, I am weak" (2 Samuel 3:39).

There will never come a moment in our life's journey when we will be without the need for mercy and grace. If we can realize that we are anointed and yet still weak, we will learn to live wisely, depending moment by moment on God's ability to keep us from sin and temptation. And for those times when we fail to abide, and find that we have sinned, the safety net of God's mercy is there to catch us, allowing him to dust us down and send us on our way again to go and sin no more.

Both grace and goodness refer to the undeserved favor that God shows to us, blessing us in many tangible ways as we journey together with him. "All the paths of the LORD are steadfast love and faithfulness" (Psalm 25:10, NRSV), and we continue to be surprised and sometimes embarrassed at his goodness. There is also the thought that God makes even the dark and difficult days somehow work into his overall plan for us, thus turning evil to good and bringing blessing out of sorrow.

It would be foolish to think that life could be nothing but pleasure and happiness. In the course of a lifetime, most of us will endure painful times, moments when we are bewildered and battered. David's assurance is that the God of grace follows hard on our heels even in such situations, to redeem and bring good out of even the most difficult of events.

A friend of mine shared recently how devastated he and his wife had been when their baby son died, just four days old. Feeling completely numb and deserted by God, he went to sit alone for a while as he sought to come to terms with the tragedy. Where was God in it all? A letter lay unopened on the table, so he picked it up to see who it was from. A friend of his, who knew nothing of the situation, had written to say that a few days earlier (at the height of the crisis) he had been burdened to pray for them, although he did not know why he should pray. He wrote to assure them of his love and, more important, of God's love. The timing of this was so amazing that my friend, despite his pain, could not escape the conclusion that even in their great loss, God was still with them and caring for them. The relentless love of God was tracking him down in his isolation and despair.

Selwyn Hughes, in his Bible reading notes on Psalm 23, speaks of his own experience of being pursued by God's relentless love. He says that in 1968 things were so bleak in his life that he considered leaving the ministry altogether. The hour of darkness proved, however, to be one of the great turning points in his life, moving him not toward a lesser ministry but toward a wider one. "Goodness and mercy followed me," he says, "and turned what looked like despair into a door of great opportunity."[17]

Hughes goes on to emphasize the importance of believing that in every event and circumstance in our lives, not only is God teaching us a great deal, but he is working to turn every loss into a gain.

While it is easy to recognize this with hindsight, it is more difficult to affirm it as we look ahead, or even as we go through certain painful periods. Nevertheless, it is a key perspective that we must develop if we are to live confidently. As Selwyn Hughes comments, "If you can get hold of this truth and absorb it into your life as a working principle, then it will transform your attitude to everything. Never again will you be at the mercy of circumstance."[18]

The journey of life has many twists and turns. There are lots of unexpected corners, roadblocks, and detours. Sometimes it seems far from straightforward, and we wonder if we will make it through. It is only when we look back that we can see how God has led us. With the value of hindsight, we can often understand why things happened as they did, recognizing how God used events and circumstances for our good. With the perspective of heaven, we will be able to see that his goodness and love were with us every step of the way.

20 Journey's End

If ever I write my autobiography (which is doubtful, because who would want to read it?) I will call it *All the Days of My Life*. I love this phrase and the thought of God's involvement in every one of my days, the assurance of his goodness and mercy pursuing me on my own particular journey. Yet within this charming title lies another, more challenging thought—the stark reminder that my days are numbered. Just as there was a beginning to my days, so there will be an end. I will not live forever.

It is easy to want to avoid the fact of our own mortality, but it is something each of us must come to terms with. One day we will die, and our life on earth will come to an end. There is a span to our lives that God has determined. On one occasion David prayed, "Show me, O Lord, my life's end and the number of my days; let me know how fleeting is my life" (Psalm 39:4). This is a healthy perspective to have on life, for it teaches us to value each day and use it well. Life is short, and it is soon over.

Those who have faced the trauma of knowing that they are terminally ill suddenly find life coming into sharper focus as they realize how short a time is left to them, and they appreciate it so much more. Like David, Moses valued that kind of insight, asking God, "Teach us to number our days aright, that we may gain a heart of wisdom" (Psalm 90:12). According to him, a normal lifespan is seventy to eighty years (Psalm 90:10), and although people in the more developed countries are living longer these days, it remains a good general guide to work on. With this as a benchmark, we can estimate roughly where we are on life's journey, and how close we are getting to its end. That is, of course, if we have a normal span of life. Not everyone does.

David seems to have faced up to his own mortality, seeing it in the light of his relationship with God. He saw death not as an end but as a beginning; not as something to be dreaded but, when the time came, as something that could be welcomed. He speaks with the same confident assurance about death as he did about life: "and I will dwell in the house of the Lord for ever." He saw death as a transition from the enjoyment of God's presence here on earth to a more complete and fuller being with him in heaven. It was simply going home.

It is hard for us to imagine what heaven is really like and why it is so much better than earth, because earth is all we know. This life is often painful and difficult, but for most of us life in general is good, and we do not want to give it up. We have a strong survival instinct. The thought of leaving it behind, and especially being separated from our loved ones, is painful and frightening. Many people fear, too, the actual process of dying, the thought of a long drawn-out and agonizing illness, the fear of the unknown.

David Watson was a well-known evangelist in England who died of cancer in 1984. His shared his personal thoughts during his struggle with the disease in a book called *Fear No Evil*. He writes openly and honestly about his ups and downs, his hope of healing, and then coming to terms with dying.

Although his faith was tested, he shared the same confident assurance of which David the psalmist spoke. He wrote:

> When I die, it is my firm conviction that I shall be more alive than ever, experiencing the full reality of all that God has prepared for us in Christ. . . . The actual moment of dying is still shrouded in mystery, but as I keep my eyes on Jesus I am not afraid. Jesus has already been through death for us, and will be with us when we walk through it ourselves.[19]

I am writing this as Easter approaches. Because Christ has died and is risen, we can have just such an assurance that death is not the end. He has defeated sin and death, and we share in his victory. To those who believe in him he gives eternal life—a quality of life that begins here and now, but that transcends the grave and continues in what the Bible calls heaven.

Recently, I attended the funeral of a man called Joe, an elderly member of our church congregation. A coal miner for much of his life, Joe was told he had lung cancer and had only months to live. Soon after he had been given the news, a friend from church visited him in hospital. When Joe shared the doctor's sad prognosis, his friend's face must have fallen, for Joe rebuked him sharply. "Don't look so upset," he said, "I'm not upset, and don't you be either!" Why was Joe not upset? Because he knew he was going home.

One of the best pieces I have read on the subject of heaven is a chapter called "Coming Home" in the book *The Sacred Romance* by Brent Curtis and John Eldredge.[20] According to them, a story is only as good as its ending, and heaven is like the end of the story, the consummation of the love story that is the relationship between God and his people. All the longings and desires of our hearts will find their fulfillment and satisfaction when we eventually arrive home, for heaven is our true home and ultimate destination. Curtis and Eldredge encourage us to use our imaginations as we dream of heaven, and suggest that heaven will offer us what we long for most—intimacy, beauty, and adventure.

All of us long for real intimacy, and it is in our love relationship with God that we can find this need most fully satisfied. The communion with God that begins on earth will be brought to its climax in heaven, when the barriers are removed and finally we can enter fully into the love that God has for us, and also fully express our love for him. This is what lies behind the thought of dwelling in the house of the Lord. It suggests that we are completely at home there, that we are relaxed and at ease. This has always been the ultimate purpose of God, to bring us into harmony with himself. In heaven that oneness will be complete.

If we think of heaven as the house of the Lord, then we know it will be a beautiful place. If the earth, which has been spoiled and ruined by sin, is so beautiful, how much more breathtaking will heaven be? Beauty is something that captivates the human heart and leads us to worship. Surrounded in heaven by all that is lovely and pure and wholesome, our hearts will rise to worship God in the beauty of holiness. Not only will we be at home with God, we shall be lost in wonder at the splendor of his dwelling place. We shall never tire of singing his praises when we see him as he is.

But worship is not the only activity of heaven. The sense of adventure that moves within us will find full expression as we begin to reign with Christ, and start to explore the wonders of the new heaven and the new earth. Heaven will not be a static place. There we shall continue to grow and develop, learning more about God, about ourselves, about each other. Far from being the end, it is really the beginning. This life is only a dress rehearsal for the real thing, which will be far, far more exciting than any of us could ever dream. As the scripture says, "No eye has seen, no ear has heard, no mind has conceived what God has prepared for those who love him" (1 Corinthians 2:9). One surprise after another awaits us. We shall never be bored, never lonely, never at a loose end. The struggles of our earthly lives will be nothing compared to the good times that God has planned for us. As David Watson said, we shall be more alive than ever.

How do we know that we will make it safe to the end? Because we have a good Shepherd to lead and to guide us. Because the king of love is escorting us. Because, as the words of Newton's great hymn "Amazing Grace" remind us, the grace of God has brought us safe this far, and that same grace will lead us home. We are sheep that are safely led, and need have no fear of falling by the wayside if we keep our eyes on Jesus.

J. D. Jones has summed up well the feeling of assurance that Psalm 23 provides.

> Those who put themselves in the care and keeping of God shall not lack for guidance, protection, provision, as they journey through life. And when life draws to its close, God's love does not fail. With God the best is always still to be. He keeps the good wine always to the last. For after seeing us safely through the valley He brings us to the house of the Lord, where faith shall become sight and dream shall become deed, and hope shall become fruition, and where every desire of the soul shall be satisfied. And in that house of the Lord we shall dwell for ever.[21]

It is neither arrogant nor presumptuous to live with such assurance. It is the gift of the gospel, the legacy of grace. Those who consciously put themselves in the care of the good Shepherd can know with certainty that death is not the end, that heaven is their destination. Without such a hope, life becomes almost unbearable, for what is the point if this life is all there is? But this is not all there is. And, as we have seen in this final reflection on Psalm 23, for those who share life's journey with a God of grace, the best is still to come.

Questions for Reflection

For individuals

1. How has God been teaching you to depend on him more? What particular blessings do you need at this time from the king's table?

2. What has been your experience of the Holy Spirit so far? How might you open yourself even more fully to his gracious ministry?

3. Do you ever feel drained and empty? If so, take some moments to lift the cup of your life prayerfully to God. Ask him to fill you to overflowing.

4. Looking back over your life, where can you see the goodness and love of God? Take a moment to express your gratitude to God.

5. Are you aware of your own mortality? How do you think of heaven? Do you have the certainty of which the psalmist David speaks?

For groups

1. How do you understand "the finished work of Christ," and how does the picture of a banqueting table illustrate it?

2. What do you think is meant by the expression "the exchanged life"?

3. How does it help to realize that you have already been anointed by the Spirit? How can we continue to live in that anointing?

4. What are the marks of an overflowing life? How can we maintain such a life?

5. Why are mercy and grace so closely linked, and why are they so important?

6. What are your thoughts about death and dying? How does Psalm 23 comfort you? How do you picture heaven in the light of what you have read?

NOTES

1. Philip Keller, *A Shepherd Looks at Psalm 23*, Pickering & Inglis, 1970, chapter 2.
2. Thomas Kelly, *A Testament of Devotion*, Harper, 1941, p. 74.
3. Selwyn Hughes, *Psalm 23*, CWR, 2001.
4. Ian Barclay, *He Is Everything to Me: An Exposition of Psalm 23*, Falcon, 1972, p. 32.
5. Marva J. Dawn, *Keeping the Sabbath Wholly: Ceasing, Resting, Embracing, Feasting*, Eerdmans, 1989, p. 60.
6. Kelly, p. 112.
7. John Ortberg, *The Life You've Always Wanted: Spiritual Disciplines for Ordinary People*, Zondervan, 1997, p. 81.
8. David Kundtz, *Stopping*, Newleaf, 1999, p. 14.
9. For an excellent survey on this problem see Alan Jamieson, *A Churchless Faith: Faith Journeys beyond the Churches*, SPCK, 2002.
10. Brennan Manning, *Ruthless Trust: The Ragamuffin's Path to God*, SPCK, 2002, p. 181.
11. J. D. Jones, *The King of Love: Meditations on the Twenty-Third Psalm*, Ambassador, 1998, p. 36.
12. Manning, p. 39.
13. Manning, p. 105.
14. R. T. Kendall, *The Anointing*, Hodder & Stoughton, 1998, p. 13.
15. F. B. Meyer, *Great Verses through the Bible*, Marshall, Morgan & Scott, 1974, p. 201.
16. *Expository Dictionary of Bible Words*, Lawrence O. Richards (ed.), Marshall Pickering, 1985, p. 439.
17. Hughes.
18. Hughes.
19. David Watson, *Fear No Evil: One Man Deals with Terminal Illness*, Hodder & Stoughton, 1984, p. 168.
20. Brent Curtis and John Eldredge, *The Sacred Romance: Drawing Closer to the Heart of God*, Nelson, 1997, pp. 177–193.
21. Jones, pp. 157–158.